Walter Camp

American Football

History, Rules, Explanations

Walter Camp

American Football
History, Rules, Explanations

ISBN/EAN: 9783742899750

Manufactured in Europe, USA, Canada, Australia, Japa

Cover: Foto ©Andreas Hilbeck / pixelio.de

Manufactured and distributed by brebook publishing software
(www.brebook.com)

Walter Camp

American Football

AMERICAN FOOTBALL

BY

WALTER CAMP

NEW AND ENLARGED EDITION

NEW YORK

HARPER & BROTHERS PUBLISHERS

1896

PREFACE

THE progress of the sport of football in this country, and a corresponding growth of inquiry as to the methods adopted by experienced teams, have prompted the publication of an enlarged edition of this book. Should any of the suggestions herein contained conduce to the further popularity of the game, the object of the writer will be attained.

CONTENTS.

EARLY AMERICAN FOOTBALL

EARLY AMERICAN FOOTBALL

FOOTBALL at American colleges runs
back beyond the memory of the oldest
living graduate. But the kind of football that was played back in the '40's
was of such a crude character that it is
hardly worthy of comment. The only
interest that attaches to it lies in the
fact that it was undoubtedly an attempt
stimulated by English ancestry to im-
plant a sport which has now grown to
remarkable prominence. In those early
days, however, it served more as an ex-
cuse for a rush between the sophomores
and the freshmen. Outside of the uni-

versities there was no football, if one
may except a New England fashion of
kicking a substitute made of a pig's
bladder in skylarking fashion after the
Thanksgiving dinner.

The football of the early college days
gave place to rushes between the classes
which were practically the same as the
football game of that day, except that
the ball was not used. These rushes,
at first governed by no laws or rules,
took on a form of organization in the
'60's, and soon after that the sport was
revived, but separate from class organi-
zations. There was no game about it
during the '60's, but a ball was kicked
about, and more or less amusement derived from it. In the early '70's, however, thanks to the inspiration of one or
two men at the various colleges — one
in particular, a former Rugby boy—the
game was taken up in earnest, and asso-

ciations organized at several of the colleges. In 1872 Columbia played a match with Yale on the 16th of November. There were twenty men on a side, and the game was nearer the English Association than the English Rugby. The costumes of the day were long trousers and jerseys. The rules were simple, and forbade any one's picking up, carrying, or throwing the ball in any part of the field. There were no "off" and "on side" rules, and goals were made by sending the ball under the cross-bar instead of over it. Fouls were penalized by making the player who had committed the foul toss the ball straight up in the air from the place where the foul occurred, and it was unfair to touch the ball until it struck the ground. This particular rule gave rise later to a good deal of skilful drop kicking, the men kicking the ball just as it touched the ground. Although the game was played with twenty men, when a man was disabled, instead of a substitute going on in his place, a man from the other side was dropped off. This was a very sensible rule, for in those days it was almost impossible to get men to try for a team ; the captain being selected more on account of his popularity and ability to get men out to the field than for any other reason. In 1873, on the 18th of October, a convention was held in New York to frame a code of rules to govern intercollegiate football. Columbia, Princeton, Rutgers, and Yale were represented. That year Princeton played a game at New Haven with Yale and defeated the New Haven men. Rutgers and Yale had a match, and Yale also played an Eton eleven, or rather an eleven formed of eleven Englishmen captained by Allen, of Eton. This

game was played at New Haven, Yale
winning by two goals to one. It was
not until 1875, however, that football
really began its present career of interest
in American colleges, when Harvard,
who had been playing matches in the
previous year with Canadian teams
under the Rugby Union rules, in a con-
ference with Yale agreed upon certain
compromise rules between the then existing American college game and the
Rugby Union. A game was played
under these rules, Harvard defeating
Yale by four goals and two touch-downs
to nothing. The principal result of the
game, however, was a thorough dissatisfaction with the compromise set of
rules, and a determination on the part
of both colleges to come to an adoption of the regular Rugby Union rules.
With the adoption of the Rugby Union
rules went out the fashions that were

existing in the American game of shouldering, or "butting" as it was called, and also the fashion of batting the ball with the hand or fist. This latter had become quite an art at one time, and men were accustomed to bat the ball in this way nearly as far as the present players kick the Rugby ball. The ball that was used in these old days was a round black rubber one, and it was "babied" with the hands a great deal. It is rather strange that this babying with the hands was adopted after many trials to acquire the knack of babying with the feet—the "dribbling" of English Association play.

ENGLISH AND AMERICAN RUGBY

AMERICAN FOOTBALL

RUGBY football—for it is from the
Rugby Union Rules that our American
Intercollegiate game was derived—dates
its present era of popularity from the
formation in England, in 1871, of a
union of some score of clubs. Nearly
ten years before this there had been
an attempt made to unite the various diverging football factions under a
common set of laws; but this proved a
failure, and the styles of play became
farther and farther apart. Of the Association game one can say but little as
regards its American following. It is

quite extensively played in this country, but more by those who have themselves played it in Great Britain than
by native-born Americans. Its popularity is extending, and at some day it
will very likely become as well understood in this country as the derived
Rugby is to-day. Its essential charac-
teristic is, that it is played with the feet,
in distinction from the Rugby, in which
the ball may be carried in the hands.

To revert to the Rugby Union.
Years before the formation of this association the game was played by sides
almost unlimited in numbers. One of
the favorite school matches was " Sixth
form against all the rest of the school."
Twenty on a side, however, became the
ruling number; but this was, after a
time, replaced by fifteens, as the days
of twenties proved only shoving matches. With the reduction in numbers

came increased running and an added interest. This change to fifteens was made in 1877, at the request of Scotland. At once there followed a more open style of play, and before long short passing became common. In 1882 the Oxford team instituted the long low pass to the open, and by the use of it remained undefeated for three seasons.

After the decrease to fifteen men the number of three-quarter-backs, who really represent our American half-backs, was increased from one to two, and two full-backs were played. A little later British captains put another full-back up into the three-quarter line, playing with only one full-back.

The Englishmen also play two men whom they call half-backs, but whose duties are like those of our quarter-back, for they seize the ball when it comes out of the scrimmage and pass it to a three-quarter for a run.

Nine men is the usual number for an English rush line, although a captain will sometimes take his ninth rusher back as a fourth three-quarter-back. There is much discussion as to when this should be done. The captain selects his men much as we do in America, and he is generally himself a player of some position behind the line, centre three-quarter being preferred. The opening play in an English Rugby game is, as a rule, a high kick well followed up. If one will bear in mind that the half backs are, like our quarter, the ones to seize the ball when it emerges from a scrimmage and pass it to the three-quarters, he will gain some idea of the character of the English method. He should understand, however, that the English half-back is obliged to look out sharply for the ball, because it comes out by chance and at random, and not directly as in our game, where the quarter can usually expect to receive the ball without trouble from the snap-back.

The forwards in an English match endeavor, when a scrimmage occurs, by kicking and pushing to drive the ball in the direction of their opponents' goal line, and they become extremely expert in the use of their feet. There are two umpires, whose duty it is to make claims (which they do by raising their flags), and a referee, who allows or disallows these claims. The penalty for fouls, which was at first only a down, is now in many cases a free kick.

The American game, it must be remembered, came from the Rugby Union in 1875, and not from the Rugby Union of to-day, although the changes in the English game have been by no manner of means commensurate with those made on this side the water. Being bound by no traditions, and having seen no play, the American took the English rules for a starting-point, and almost immediately proceeded to add and subtract, according to what seemed his pressing needs. And they were many. A favored few, whose intercourse with Canadian players had given them some of the English ideas, were able to explain the knotty points to a small degree, but not enough to really assist the mass of uninitiated players to an understanding. Misinterpretations were so numerous as to render satisfactory rulings almost out of the question and explanatory legislation imperative. In the autumn of 1876 the first game under Rugby rules between American colleges was played at New Haven, and before another was attempted a convention had tried its hand at

correcting the weak points, as they ap-
peared to the minds of the legislators,
in the Rugby Union Rules.

The feature of the American game in
distinction from the English is, just as
it was within a year from the time of
the adoption of the sport, the *outlet of
the scrimmage.*

In this lies the backbone to which the
entire body of American football is at-
tached.   The English half-backs stand
outside the scrimmage, and when the ball
pops out it is their duty to seize it and
pass it out to a three-quarter, who runs
with it.   The American quarter-back
stands behind the scrimmage and gives
a signal, immediately after which he
knows the ball will come directly into
his hands to be passed for a run or a
kick.   What is, therefore, in the English
game a matter of considerable chance
is "cut-and-dried" in the American

2

game ; and the element of chance being eliminated, opportunity is given for the display in the latter game of far more skill in the development of brilliant plays and carefully planned manœuvres.

The Americans started with the English scrimmage, kicked at the ball, and pushed and scrambled for a season, until it was discovered that a very clever manifestation of the play was to let the opponents do the kicking—in fact, to leave an opening at the proper moment through which the ball would come, and a man a few feet behind this opening could always get the ball and pass it while the men who kicked it were still entangled in the scrimmage. After a little of this, no one was anxious to kick the ball through, and the rushers began to roll the ball sidewise along between the lines. Then almost immediately it was discovered that a man could snap the ball backwards with his toe, and the American outlet was installed.

At first the play was crude in the extreme, but even in its earliest stages it proved distinctly more satisfactory to both player and spectator than the kicking and shoving which marked the English method.

The same man did not always snap the ball back as he does now, but any one of the rushers would do it upon occasion. The men did not preserve their relative positions in the line, and any one of the men behind the line would act as a quarter-back. Such a condition of affairs could not, however, last long where intercollegiate rivalry proved such an incentive to the perfection of play, and the positions of centre-rush or snapback and quarter-back became the most distinctive of any upon the field. The centre-rush at that time was selected

more for his agility, strange to say, than
for his weight and strength ; but in case
he was a light man he was always flanked
by two heavy guards.   One season's play
convinced all captains that the centre
section of the forward line must be
heavy, and if any light-weights were to
be used among the rushers they should
be near the wings.

Quarter-back has, from the very outset, been a position in which a small man
can be used to great advantage. The half-
backs and backs have usually been men
of speed coupled with skill as kickers.

The number originally adopted for
matches in this country was eleven on
a side.   From some silly notion that it
would increase the skill displayed, this
number was changed to fifteen, although
the Englishmen were moving in the
other direction by reducing their numbers from twenties to fifteens. A year

or two of fifteen on a side drove the American players back to elevens, and there the number has rested.

In the early days of the sport, while the players individually were courageous, the team play was cowardly; that is, the tacticians were so taken up with a study of defence—how to protect the goal—that the attack was weak. The direct result of this was to place too few men in the forward line and too many behind it. If to-day we were to revert to fifteen on a side, there is little doubt that we should throw eleven of them up into the rush line, and upon occasion even twelve. We now realize that the best defence does not consist in planning how to stop a man after he has obtained a fair start towards the goal, but in throwing all available force up against him before he can get free of the forward line. The only way to effectively defeat this aggressive defence is by means of skilled kicking. It is possible with really good kickers to throw a team playing in this fashion into disorder by well-placed and long punting, followed up most sharply; but it requires nerve and an unfailing accuracy of aim and judgment. The alterations in the playing rules, adopted lately, go far towards increasing the value of kicking, and make it imperative for a team to learn the kicking game.

It is only a few years ago that it required considerable argument to convince a captain that he could with safety send one of his halves up into the forward line when his opponents had the ball; but it will take better kicking than is exhibited in most of the championship matches to frighten that halfback out of the line now. Even the quarter was wont upon occasion to drop back among the halves and assist them rather than the rushers.

All the tendency for the last few years has been towards diminishing the number of men held in reserve, as it were, behind the line, and increasing by this means the crushing force by which the forwards might check either runner or kicker before his play could be executed.

Should the English ever adopt an outlet for their scrimmage, making the play as direct as is ours, their men would gravitate to the forward line as rapidly as have our players.

Next to the difference in scrimmage outlet between our game and that of the British stands a much more recent development, which we call interference. This is the assistance given to a runner by a companion or companions who go before him and break a path for him or shoulder off would-be tacklers. This, to the Englishman, would be the most detestable kind of off-side play, and not tolerated for an instant upon any field in the United Kingdom.

Even into this the Americans did not plunge suddenly, but rather little by little they stepped in, until it was necessary to do one of two things — either legalize what was being tacitly consented to, or penalize it heavily. The result was that it was legalized. With this concession, though, there went a certain condition which gained a measure of confidence for the new ruling.

To understand just how this state of affairs above mentioned came about one should know that, in the attempt to block opponents when the quarter-back was receiving and passing the ball, the forwards fell into the habit of extending their arms horizontally from the shoulder, as by this method each man

could cover more space. For a number
of years this went on without detriment
to the sport in any way, but after a
time there was more or less complaint
of holding in the line, and it was ruled
that a man must not change his position
after the ball was snapped, nor bend his
arms about an opponent at such a time.
Unfortunately the referee (for at this
stage of the game there was no umpire)
could not watch the ball and the players with sufficient care to enforce this
ruling, and the temper of the players
suffered accordingly. It is always the
case when a rule is not enforced un-
flinchingly, no matter from what cause,
that both sides suffer, and the tendency
always is towards devising additional in-
fringements. The additional infringement in this instance was even worse
than could have been foreseen ; for, not
content with simply blocking or even

holding an opponent until the quarter should have passed the ball in safety, the players in the forward line saw an opportunity for going a step farther, and actually began the practice of seizing an opponent long after the ball had been played, and dragging him out of the way of the running half-back. In the thick of the rush line this was frequently possible without risk of discovery by the referee; and, emboldened by successes of this kind, men would reach out even in the open, and drag back a struggling tackler just as he was about to lay his hands upon the runner. It was this state of affairs which brought up the question, " How much should a comrade be allowed to aid the runner?"

American football legislators answered this question satisfactorily for the time, after long discussion, by determining

that the runner might be assisted to
any extent, provided the assistant did
not use his hands or arms in performing
this office. The first result of this was
to lower the arms of the rushers when
lined up, and, in spite of some forebod-
ings, this proved really a benefit to the
game. The second result has been to
perfect a system of flanking a runner
by companions who form almost an im-
passable barrier at times to the would-
be tacklers. But a new element came
in after a while in the shape of what
were called momentum - mass plays.
The development of the interference
phase became so great that it was
the custom to group a body of men
at some distance from the line — several yards — and then start this mass
in motion before the ball was put in
play. The opponents were unable to
go forward to meet this mass, on

account of the danger of getting off-side, and so were taken at no inconsiderable disadvantage. This became such a dangerous as well as uninteresting method of play in the minds of the public that legislation was begun against it.

At the same time with mention of the solution of this problem, one should also call attention to a menace which threatened American football far more seriously than did this; and that, too, at a time when the sport was by no means so strong in years or popularity as when this later difficulty arose. I refer to the " block game." This method of play, which consisted in a succession of " downs " without advance and without allowing the opponents any chance of securing possession of the ball, proved a means by which a weak team could avoid defeat. The whole object of the

match was thus frustrated, the game re-
sulting in no score.

To meet this difficulty a rule was introduced making it incumbent upon a
side to advance the ball five yards or retreat with it ten in three "downs."   If
this advance or retreat were not accomplished, the ball went at once into the
possession of the opponents.   Never
did a rule in any sport work so immediate and satisfactory a reform as did this
five-yard rule.

Within the last few years, up to 1894,
there had been no important change in
the conduct of the American game, nor
in the rules.   Out of the above-men-
tioned points of difference between it
and the English game, there is only that
of the methods of enforcing rules and
determining differences.   The English
have a referee and two umpires, although the umpires are sometimes re-

placed by touch-judges. The umpires
act, as did the judges in our game of
ten years ago, as advocates for their re-
spective sides, and it is this advocacy
which is causing them to fall into dis-
favor there exactly as they did here.
Touch-judges merely watch the lines of
the field, and decide when and where
the ball goes into touch. In cases
where they are employed, the referee
renders all decisions upon claim of the
captains. In our method there is a division of labor, but along different lines.
Our three officials, the umpire, referee,
and linesman, have their separate prov-
inces, the first ruling upon the conduct of
players as to off-side and other offences,
while the second determines questions
of fact as to when the ball is held or
goes into touch, also whether a goal is
kicked or not. As the rule has it, the
umpire is judge for the players, and the

referee for the ball. The linesman was added in 1894, and his duties are to mark the distances gained and lost in the progress of the play, to keep the time, and to bear testimony, as do also the other officials, when asked as to the offences of roughness, off-side play, and holding.

The American rules, owing to the above - mentioned dissatisfaction with the undue development of interference and the consequent exaggeration of mass and push-plays to the detriment of kicking and open running, were altered in 1894 through the instrumentality of the University Athletic Club of New York City. The principal changes which were then made were as follows : Momentum - mass plays were forbidden, and not more than three men were allowed even to start before the ball was put in play. An especial inducement was also offered for drop-kicking by the passage of a rule providing that when a side tried a drop-kick at goal upon any first-down inside the opponent's twenty-five yard line and the result was a touch-back, the attacking side could then line up at kick-out upon the ten yard line instead of, as formerly, at the twenty-five-yard line.

A rule was also passed providing for greater protection to a man making a fair catch. But perhaps the principal alteration, and the one bringing about far more kicking than had been practised for many years on this side the water, was that enforcing an actual kick of at least ten yards in every case where the rules provide for a kick. Instead of the inevitable wedge seen upon American fields for years at every kick-off, kick-out, and free-kick, there is now a vigorous drive made, and the play opened up for a time at least. With this change have come in many modifications attractive to both player and spectator.

In 1896 the Rules Committee of the University Athletic Club made further restrictions upon momentum plays by enacting a rule that forbade any man to be in motion when the ball was put in play save a single man, who could be running towards his own goal. They also legislated against mass playing by practically compelling five men to be in the rush line ; and in case of five men besides the quarter dropping back, two were obliged to separate or stand outside the end men of the line, or else drop back at least five yards.

END RUSHER

THE end rusher must get into condition early. Unless he does, he cannot handle the work that must fall to his share, and the effect of a poor performance by the end is to produce disorder at once in the proportion of work as well as the quality of the work of the tackles and half-backs. This is not well understood by captains and coaches, but it is easy to see if one follows the play. A tired end rusher, even one who has experience and a good idea of his place, will lope down the field under a kick, and by his lack of speed will allow a return; and, against a running game, while he will, it is true, force his man in, he will do it so slowly that the runner is enabled to pass the tackle. The first will surely result in his own backs shortening their kicks, and the second in drawing his own tackle too widely from the guard. Both these results seriously affect the value of the practice for backs and tackles; consequently, the end must be put in condition early. The finer points of his position can be worked up gradually, but his endurance must be good at the outset, in order that the others may become accustomed to rely upon him for regular work. But it sometimes happens that the captain or coach has no chance to make sure of this. His candidates may be raw, and only appear upon the first day of fall practice. In that case there is a method which he can adopt to advantage, and which answers the purpose. It is to play his candidates for that position one after the other in rotation, insisting upon hard playing even if it be for only five minutes at a time. In this way not only will the tackle receive the proper support, but the ends themselves will improve far more rapidly than under the usual method. Every player upon a team has to labor under two distinctly different sets of circumstances: one set arising from the possession of the ball by his opponents, and the other from the possession of the ball by his own side. Many an error in instruction or coaching arises from terming the tactics adopted under these two conditions defensive and offensive. It is no uncommon thing to see an end rusher, who has been told that such and such is his defensive play, so affected by the word *defensive*, as applied to his action, as to fail entirely to perform any aggressive work when his opponents have the ball. And a similarly undesirable state of affairs is brought about by the term *offensive* when his own side have the ball. In this latter case, he seems inspired to become aggressive in his conduct towards his opponent from the moment the men are lined up, and this very often leads him to make any interference of his so premature as to render it useless towards favoring his runner. One of the first things, therefore, for a coach to tell an end rusher is that the terms offensive and defensive, as applied to team work, have nothing to do with the aggressiveness of any individual. Then, as a matter of still better policy, let him avoid using these terms in individual coaching.

When the opponents have the ball, the end rusher must, in the case of a kick, do his utmost to prevent his *vis-à-vis* from getting down the field early under the ball, and he should stay with him until his own back has secured the ball. That is the cardinal point, and it is not necessary for him to do much thinking regarding anything else when he is facing a kicking game. When his opponents are about to make a run, the situation is much more involved. He must then consider himself as the sole guardian of that space of ground extending from his tackle to the edge of the field, and he must begin at the touch line and work in. That is, he must remember that, while on one side of him there is the tackle, who will do his utmost to help him out, there is on the other side—that is, towards touch— no one to assist him, and a run around the end means a free run for many yards. "Force the man in" is always a good motto for an end, and one he will do well to follow conscientiously. To force the man in does not mean, however, to stand with one foot on the touch line, and then reach in as far as possible and watch the man go by, as nine out of every ten ends have been doing for some years. It means, go at the runner with the determination of getting him any way, but taking him always from the outside. An end cannot tackle as occasionally does a half-back or back, slowly and even waiting for his man, then meeting him low and strong. An end always has to face interference, and good interference will bowl over a waiting end with ease. An end must go up as far and fast as he dares to meet the runner, and when his moment comes—which must be a selected moment—he must shoot in at his man, reaching him, if possible, with his shoulder, and at the same time extending his arms as far around him as possible. Many times this reaching enables an end to grasp his man even though a clever interferer break the force of his tackle. And when his fingers touch the runner, he must grip with the tenacity of the bull-dog, and never let go.

It seems almost unnecessary to say that a high tackler has no chance what-ever as an end rusher. He may play guard or centre, but before a man ever es-says the end he must have passed through all the rudimentary schooling in tackling, and be such an adept that to pass him without the assistance of the most clever interference is an impossibility.

An end should be a good follower; that is, if the runner make in towards the tackle, the end should run him down from behind when interference cuts off the tackle. This is one of the best points for cultivation, because it effect-ually prevents any dodging by the run-ner. If he fail to take his opening cleanly, a following end is sure of him. This is not a safe point, however, to teach until the player has fairly mastered the ordinary end-work; for the tendency is to leave his own position too soon, giving the runner an opportunity to turn out behind him, and thus elude the tackle without difficulty.

A few years ago there was quite a fashion for the man putting the ball in from touch to run with it along the edge of the field. The alteration in the rule regarding a fair has now, however, entirely done away with this play. Of these close double passes at the edge of the field the most effective were those wherein the runner darted by just inside the touch line, and the weakest the ones wherein the attempt was made to advance out into the field. To the players in the centre of the line there is no apparent difference under the new rules.

To the end and tackle, however, the difference is marked, because the man in putting the ball in play from a fair can no longer run with it, but must either kick it or walk in and have it down. The instructions to the end are, therefore, to be sure to get to the spot in time to prevent a kick. One can be quite sure that the opponents will not play the ball from touch unless they have time enough for a satisfactory kick. Without such it is by far the better policy to walk out the fifteen paces and have it down. When his own side have possession of the ball, the end rusher's play, like that of any other man, must be governed by the character of the intended move, and the knowledge of what this move will be is conveyed to him by the signal. The nearer the play is to his end, the greater is the assistance he can render. There is little need of coaching him to do his

work when the run is along his line, nor,
in fact, when it is upon his side of the
centre. The knowledge of the proximity of the runner stirs him up sufficiently, if he have any football blood in
him. The point towards which coaching
should be directed and where it is needed is in starting instantly to render
assistance when the play is upon the
other side of the line. There is no
limit to the amount of work an end
may perform in this direction. A good
end can toss his man back so that he
cannot interfere with the play, and then
cross over so quickly as to perform
effective interference even upon end
runs. In " bucking the centre" he can
come from behind with valuable weight
and pressure. Dropping the ends back
has come to be a favorite move in these
days of wedge work, and will not by
any means be discarded under the

later rules. A coach should remember, though, that it will not do to start an end into doing too much unless he is able to stand the work, for an end had better do the work well upon his own side than be only half-way useful upon both ends. A tired-out end makes the opponents doubly strong.

With the increase in the number of kicks there has come a greater necessity of fast and untiring runners for the wings. To get down under a kick is the great feature, and while the tackles are taking up a great deal of this duty, the end still has far more of it than any untrained or poorly conditioned man can stand or perform satisfactorily.

THE TACKLE

THE TACKLE

THOSE teams upon which the work of end and tackle has been best developed have, for the last few years, been markedly superior in the opposition offered to plays of their opponents. This fact in itself is an excellent guide to the style of play one ought to expect from these two positions. The four men occupying them are the ones to meet nine tenths of the aggressive work of the opponents, unless in the exaggerated use of centre wedges, and the rules adopted lately have curtailed that. The position of end has already been dwelt upon at length. That of tackle, a position much later to reach the full stage of development than the end, has nevertheless now attained quite an equal prominence. The tackle is an assistant to both end and guard, while he has also duties of his own demanding constant attention.

When the opponents have the ball and are about to kick, the tackle is one of the most active components of the line. He may not be moving until the ball is snapped, but upon the instant that it is played he is at work. He may himself go through to prevent the pass or kick, or he may make a chance for a line half-back to do this. By a line half-back is meant one who, upon his opponents' plays, comes up into the line and performs the duties of a rusher. This method has become so common of late that it is well understood. The play of this line half-back must dovetail into the work of the tackle so well as to make their system one of thoroughly mutual understanding. For this reason they should do plenty of talking and planning together off the field, and carry their plans into execution in daily practice until they become in company a veritable terror to opponents, particularly to kicking backs.

One of the very simple, yet clever and successful, combinations worked in this way has been for the line half to take his position outside the tackle, who immediately begins to edge out towards the end. This opens a gap between the opposing tackle and guard, for the tackle will naturally follow his man. This line half simply watches the centre, and as he sees the ball played goes sharply behind the tackle and through the opening. This play can be greatly aided by cleverness on the part of the tackle, who, to perform it to perfection, should edge out most cautiously, and with an evident intention of going to the outside of his man. He should also watch the centre play, and, most important of all, jump directly forward into his man when the ball is snapped. This will enable the half to take almost a direct line for the back, and with his flying start have more than a fair chance of spoiling the kick. The tackle must not be idle after his plunge, but should follow in sharply, because there will always be an opposing half protecting the kicker; and if the line half be checked by this man, as is not unlikely, the following tackle has an excellent opportunity by getting in rapidly. The tackle and half should alternate in their arrangement, neither one always going through first, and thus add to the anxiety and discomfort of the opponents.

When the opponents are about to run instead of kick, the same combination of line half and tackle can be put in operation, except that it will not do for these two to follow each other through with such freedom, as there is too much danger of both being shunted off by a clever turn coupled with well-timed interference. The cardinal point to be remembered is, to be far enough apart so that a single dodge and one interference cannot possibly throw off both men.

The tackle's duties towards the end have been partially described in dwelling upon the work of the latter, but there is plenty of detail to be studied. One of the first things to impress upon the tackle is, that he must watch the ball, not only upon the pass from the quarter, but also after it settles in the runner's arms, for the most successful double or combination passes are those which draw the tackle in towards the centre and give the second recipient of the ball only the end to pass. It has been too common a mistake of coaches to caution a tackle who has been deceived by this double pass against "going so hard." This is wrong. It soon results in making a slow man of the player, for he hangs back to see if the runner be not about to pass the ball, until he is too late to try for the man before he reaches the rush line; and, with the present system of interference and crowding a runner after he reaches the rush line, there is no chance to stop him short of three, and it may very likely be five, yards. The proper coaching is to send him through on the jump, with his eyes open for tricks. Let him take a step or two towards the runner, so that, if no second pass be made, the tackle will be sure to meet him before he reaches the rush line, and not after it. This method of coaching makes not only sharp tackles, but quick and clever ones, with plenty of independence, which will be found a most excellent quality.

As regards the relations between the tackle and guard, they are best defined by saying that the guard expects to receive the assistance of the tackle in all cases requiring agility, while in cases requiring weight the guard is equally ready to lend assistance to the tackle.

When his own side has the ball, the tackle has far more than the end to do. In fact, the tackle has the most responsible work of any man along the line, having more openings to make, and at the same time the blocking he has to perform is more difficult. The earlier description of the work of a line half and the tackle in getting through is sufficient to indicate the difficulties which the opposing tackle must face in preventing this breaking through.

While blocking may not be the most important duty, it is certainly the one which will bear the most cultivation in the tackles of the present day, for the ones who are really adept in it are marked exceptions to the general run. It is no exaggeration to say that more than two thirds of the breaking through that does real damage comes between the end and guard, and therefore in the space supposed to be under the care of the tackle. By successful blocking is meant, not unfair holding, which sooner or later will result in disaster, nor backing upon a runner or kicker as the charger advances, which is almost as bad as no blocking, but that clever and properly timed body-checking of the opponent which delays him just long enough to render his effort to reach his man futile every time. This kind of blocking looks so easy, and is so difficult, that it is found only in a

man who is willing to make a study of
it. Coaching can but give any one wish-
ing to acquire this a few points; the real
accomplishment depends upon the man's
unflagging perseverance and study. The
first thing to be noted is, that a really
good forward cannot possibly be blocked
every time in the same way. He soon
becomes used to the method, and is able
to avoid the attempt. Dashing violently
against him just as he is starting may
work once or twice, and then he will
make a false start to draw this charge,
and easily go by the man. Standing
motionless, and then turning with a
sharp swing back against him, will disconcert his charge once in a while. Shouldering him in the side as he passes will
throw him off his balance or against
some other man, if well performed, occasionally. Falling down before him
by a plunge will upset him even when

he has quite a clear space apparently, but it will not work if played too often. By a preconcerted plan he may be coaxed through upon a pretended snap, and then the ball played while he is guarded and five yards gained by his off-side play, but he will not be taken in again by the same method. Nor is this quite in the proper spirit of the sport. These are but a few of the strategies which engage the study of the tackle. How soon to let the man through is also an important question. When the ball is to be punted, the tackle upon the kicker's side must block long and hard, while the tackle upon the other end should block sharply, and then let his man through for the sake of getting down the field under the kick. When a drop is to be attempted, the blocking upon both sides must be close and long, much longer than for a punt. Moreover, it is by no means a bad policy to have the blocking last until the ball is actually seen in the air in front of the line, because then, if the kick be stopped, the tackles can go back to assist the backs in recovering the ball. The blocking for a kick, as a rule, should be close; that is, every opponent must be matched from the centre out, leaving the free man or men on the ends. This rule has its exceptions, but when there is any doubt about the play it is safest to block close, and take the chances from the ends rather than through breaks in the line.

In blocking for a run the case is very different, and depends upon the point of assault. If the run is to be made around the right end, for instance, by the left half-back, the right tackle must block very slowly and long. That is, he must not dash up to his man the instant the ball is snapped and butt him aside, for the runner will not be near enough to derive any advantage from this, and the opponent will easily recover in time to tackle him. Rather should he avoid contact with his man until his runner makes headway, and then keep between the opponent and runner until the latter puts on steam to circle, when it is his duty to engage his man sharply, and thus let the runner pass. In blocking for an inside run upon his own side, he should turn his man out or in, as the case may be, just as the runner reaches the opening, being particularly careful not to make the break too early, lest the opponent reach the runner before he comes to the opening.

A few words of comment upon the principles of momentum - mass plays should be given, even though the present rules are directed against them. It is hardly probable that the principle involved will be wholly given up, although the methods will be more or less altered. The real momentum-mass play depended upon bringing a group of men in motion against a man or men compelled, through fear of off-side, to stand still. Thus three or four men would form in the shape of a line or wedge some eight or ten yards back of the spot where the ball was down, and not until they were in full tilt at the opposing line would the ball be played. The over-development of this play has brought about its condemnation. Momentum plays have now been practically abolished, but mass plays are still in vogue, and on these a tackle's duty is mainly to smash or check the progress of the mass, throwing the weight back upon the runner, or forcing him to come out so that the end rush line, half, or guard may reach him.

THE GUARD

THE GUARD

THE position of guard, while it requires less agility than that of tackle, can never be satisfactorily filled by a man who is slow. Many a coach makes this mistake and fails to see his error until too late to correct it. I remember once seeing upon a minor team a guard who weighed at least 190 pounds replaced by a man of 155, and the latter actually filled the position—greatly to my astonishment, I confess—in excellent fashion. This does not at all go to prove that weight is of no value in a guard. On the contrary, it is a quality especially to be desired, and if one can find a heavy man who is not slow he is the choice by all means. But weight must be given work to do, and that work demands practice, and slowness of execution cannot be tolerated. At the outset the coach must impress this fact upon the guards, and insist upon their doing their work quickly. It is really wonderful how much better the effect of that work will prove to be when performed with a snap and dash that are not difficult to acquire.

When the opponents have the ball and are about to kick, the guard should have in his mind one persistent thought, and that is, to reach the quarter before the ball is away from his hand, but not to stop there. It is only once in a great while that fortune favors sufficiently to crown this attempt with success. When it does, so much the better; but the guard should take in the quarter only in a general sweep, making on for the kicker, and at the same time getting

his arms up in the air when he comes
before him, so as to take every possible
chance of stopping the ball. Just here
it may be well to explain the confidence
with which in these details of coaching
the phrases are used "when the opponents are about to kick" and "when
the opponents are about to run." It
is true that one cannot tell infallibly
every time whether the play will be a
kick or a run, but experienced players
are really so seldom at fault in their
judgment upon this point that it is safe
to coach as though there never existed
any doubt about the matter.

To continue with the work of the
guard when the opponents are about to
attempt a run. One of the most important features of the play in this position is to guard against small wedges.
If a guard simply stands still and
straight he will be swept over like a

wisp of straw by any well-executed wedge play directed at him. An experienced man knows this, and his chief thought is how to avoid it, and how, first, to prevent the formation; second, to alter the direction, and, finally, to stop the progress, of this terror of centre work, the small wedge. There are as many ways of accomplishing these results as of performing the duties of tackle or end, and it rests with the individual player to study them out. To prevent the formation of small wedges, the most successful method is that of sudden and, if possible, disconcerting movements. Jostling, so far as it is allowed, sudden change of position, a pretended charge — all these tend to break up the close formation. Once formed and started, the change of direction is usually the most disarranging play possible; but this should not be attempted by the player or players opposite the point of the wedge. At that spot the proper play is to check advance, even temporarily; for the advance once checked, the wedge may be swung from the side so as to take off the pressure from behind. So it is the men at the side who must endeavor to turn the wedge and take off this pressure. Without the actual formation upon the field it is difficult to fully explain this turning of the wedge; but if the principle of the defence be borne in mind, it will not be found so hard to understand. Check the peak even for a moment, and get the weight off from behind as speedily as possible. The men who are pushing must necessarily act blindly; and if their force is not directly upon the men at the point of the V, they pass by the man with the ball and so become useless. Both guards must keep their weight down low, close to the ground, so that the wedge, if directed at either, cannot throw that one at once off his balance backward. If this occurs, the wedge will always make its distance, perhaps go many yards. Lying down before the wedge is a practice based upon this principle of keeping close to the ground, and is by no means an ineffectual way of stopping an advance, although it is not as strong a play as bringing about the same result without actually losing the power to straighten up if the wedge turns. Moreover, the men in the front of a wedge are becoming so accustomed to meeting this flat defence that they not infrequently succeed in getting over the prostrate man and regaining headway upon the other side. This, as one can readily see, must always yield a very considerable gain. When a run is attempted at some other point in the line, it is the duty of the guards to get through hard and follow the runner into his opening, even if they cannot reach him before he comes into the line. In this class of play a guard should remember that if he can lay a hand upon the runner before he reaches the line he can spoil the advance to a certainty, for no runner can drag a heavy guard up into and through an opening. It is like dragging a heavy and unwieldy anchor. A guard can afford to, and must sometimes, tackle high. Not that he should, in the open, ever go at the shoulders, but in close quarters he often has no time to get down low, and must make the best of taking his man anywhere that the opportunity offers. He must always, however, throw him towards the opponent's goal. Another point for guards to bear in mind is, that in close

quarters it is often possible to deprive
the runner of the ball before he says
" down." A guard who always tries
this will be surprised at the number of
times he will find the referee giving him
the ball. He will also be astonished at
the way this attempt results in the runner saying " down " as soon as he finds
some one tugging at the ball. A man
gives up all thought of further advance
the instant he finds the ball slipping at
all in his grasp; and when his attention
is distracted from the idea of running,
as it is when he is fearful of losing the
ball, he can never make use of his opportunities to good advantage. For
this reason the coach should impress
upon all the forwards the necessity of
always trying to take away the ball;
but the men in and near the centre
are likely to have the best opportunity
for this play, because it is there that

the runner encounters a number of men
at once rather than a single individual.

When his own side have the ball the
guard must block sharply until the
quarter has time for receiving the ball,
and, at any rate, beginning the motion of
the pass. It is safer, in the case of inexperienced guards, to tell them to block
until the quarter has time to get rid of
the ball. The distinction is this: that
an experienced guard sometimes likes
to gain just that second of time between the beginning of the pass and
the completion of the swing, and utilize
it in getting down the field or into the
interference. So accustomed does he
become to measuring the time correctly
that he will let the opponent through
just too late to reach the quarter, although it seems a very close call. It is
not safe to let green guards attempt
anything so close. They must be

taught to block securely until the ball is on its way to the runner or kicker. The blocking of a guard is much less exacting in its requirements than that of the tackle. Not that he must not block with equal certainty, but the act requires seldom such covering of two men as often happens in the case of a tackle. The quarter will very likely come up, but he can be on but one side at a time, and he is also usually a light man. The guard forms closely towards the centre, and then follows his man out if he moves out, but only as far as he can go, and still be absolutely certain that the opponent cannot pass between him and the snap-back. To be drawn or coaxed out far enough to admit of an opponent's going through the centre shows woful ignorance in any guard.

When a kick is to be made the blocking must be prolonged a little, and on a drop-kick (as mentioned earlier) it should last until the ball goes from the foot. When blocking for a run, of course much depends upon where the opening is to be made, and a guard must be governed accordingly. The method itself is, again, different in the guard from that exhibited in the tackle. A guard may not move about so freely and must face his man more squarely than a tackle, for the guard must protect the quarter first, while the tackle considers the half only. If a guard allows his opponent to get a fair lunge with outstretched arm over or past his shoulder, he may reach the quarter's arm even though his body is checked, while such a reach at the point in the line occupied by the tackle would be of no value whatever. It was once the duty of the guards, previous to the snap-back's playing the ball, to see that their individual opponents did not succeed in either kicking the ball out from the snap-back's hand or otherwise interfering with his play. A rule has now been made, however, which saves the guards this trouble; still a centre should always feel that he has upon either hand a steady and wide-awake assistant, who will neither be caught napping nor allow any unfair advantage to be taken of him. The guard should bear in mind one fact, however, and that most clearly. It is that squabbling and general pushing about are far more liable to disconcert his own centre and quarter than to interfere with the work of the opponents.

THE CENTRE, OR SNAP-BACK

THE man who may be selected to fill the important position of centre-rush must be a man of sense and strength. Brain and brawn are here at their highest premium. But there is another element of character without which both will be overthrown, and that is patience. Practical experience has taught football coaches that none but a thoroughly self-controlled man can make a success in football in any position, while in this particular one his disposition should be of the most equable nature. He will be called upon to face all kinds of petty annoyances, for his opponents will endeavor to make his play as difficult as possible; and never must he al-

low himself for one instant to lose sight
of the fact that his entire attention
must be devoted to his play, and none
of it distracted by personal feeling.
Moreover, while he must be able to
play the ball quickly when called upon,
he can never afford to be hurried by his
opponents.   With the present excellent
rulings of umpires regarding interference with the ball before it is snapped,
much of the most harassing kicking of
the ball from under his hand has been
stopped ; but, for all that, he is indeed a
lucky centre who does not feel the ball
knocked out from under his grasp several times during a game.   In addition
to this, every man who breaks through
gives him a rub.   Sometimes these
knocks are intentional, often they are
given purely by accident, and the latter
are by no means the lightest.   Then,
too, a man is pushed into the snap-back

just as the ball goes. It may be his own guard, but the blow hurts just as much; and a centre who is not amiable under such treatment soon loses his head and forgets that he should care for nothing except to accomplish gains for his own side. The object of placing so much stress upon this qualification is to impress upon a coach the almost inestimable value of the quality of patience in any men he may be trying for this position. He can never say too much about it.

As regards the duties of the place, they differ from those of any other position in the line on account of the constant presence at that spot of the ball. The centre is either playing the ball himself or watching his antagonist play the ball at every down; so that while he has all the other duties of a forward to execute, he has the special work besides.

Here is the weakness of so many centres. They are snap-backs only or forwards only, the former being by all odds the more common. A good critical coach of experience will see nine out of every ten men whom he may watch in this position playing through day after day with no more idea of doing any forward work than if they were referees. Putting the ball in play at the right time, and properly, is a great achievement, but it does not free the centre-rush from all other obligations. He must protect his quarter; he must aid in making openings, and perform any interference that may be possible, as well as always assisting a runner of his own side with weight or protection. He must sometimes get down the field under a kick, for it is by no means unusual for him to have the best opportunity in these days when end rushers are so carefully watched. When the opponents have the ball, he must not be content with seeing that the opponent does not roll it to a guard, but must also see that there is no short, tricky passing in the scrimmage. Then he must be as ready as either guard to meet, stop, or turn a wedge. He must make openings for his comrades to get through, even when he himself may be blocked, and always be ready to reach out or throw himself before a coming runner to check the advance.

The details of the special work of the centre are many, and thorough knowledge of them can only come from experience. During his early progress a new snap-back usually sends the ball against his own legs, or, if he manages to keep them out of the way, is upset by his opponent for his pains. It is no child's play to hold a ball out at arm's-

length on the ground in front of one
and roll it back so that it passes between one's feet, and still preserve a
good balance in spite of a sudden push
of a hundred-and-eighty-pound opponent. But that is just what a centre has
to do every time the ball is down and
belongs to his side. The first thing to
teach a centre is to stand on his feet
against any amount of jostling. Then
he must learn to keep possession of the
ball until ready to play it. Both of
these acquirements take practice. The
most finished and experienced centres
have a way of playing the ball just as
they are half straightening as though
to meet a charge from in front. This
insures their not being pushed over on
to the quarter, and yet does not cause
them to lean so far forward as to be
pitched on their noses by a little assistance from the opposing centre. When

a man stands so as to prevent a push in the chest from upsetting him, he naturally puts one foot back some distance as a support. When a centre does this he is apt to put that foot and leg in the path of the ball. A second objection to this way of standing is, that the centre does not offer nearly as much opposition to any one attempting to pass as he does when he stands more squarely faced about with a good spread of the legs. As to holding the ball, some centres prefer to take it by the end, while others roll it on its side. It can be made to rise for the quarter if sent on end, whereas if played upon its side it lies closer to the ground. The quarter's preference has, therefore, something to do with it. It requires longer practice and more skill to play the ball on its end, but it permits an umpire to see more clearly whether the ball be

actually put in play by the snap-back
or played for him by the surreptitious
kick of the opponent. It has also the
advantage of sending the ball more nar-
rowly upon a line, so that its course is less
likely to be altered than when rolled
upon its side. While the snap-back is
seldom held to the very strictest con-
formity to the rule about being on side
when he puts the ball in play, it is necessary for him to practise with a view
to this particular, because he is liable to
be obliged to conform every time if the
opponents insist. The reason for care-
lessness in this respect is this: There is
no penalty for infringement except that
of being obliged to return to the spot
and put the ball in play properly. A
certain laxity, therefore, is granted rather than delay the play. But, as stated
above, a centre must be able to put the
ball in play when fairly on side, and must

live up to this with some moderate degree of regularity, or else the umpire will call an off side and bring him back. A centre ought to practise putting the ball in play with either hand until he is fairly proficient with his left as well as his right. Not that he should use his hands alternately in a game, but that an injury to his right hand need not necessarily throw him out of the game. It is by no means an unrecognized fact that the greater amount of experience possessed by the regular centre is so valuable as to make it policy to keep him in his place so long as his legs are good, even though a hand be injured, rather than to replace him by the substitute with whose methods the quarterback is not so familiar.

A coach should see to it that his centre has a variety of men to face, some big, some tricky, some ugly. If any old play-

ers come back to help the team in the
way of coaching, and among them are
some centre rushers, they can do no better work than by donning a uniform and
playing against the " 'Varsity " centre.

THE QUARTER-BACK

THE quarter is, under the captain, the director of the game. With the exception of one or two uncommon and rare plays, there is not one of any kind, his side having the ball, in which it does not pass through his hands. The importance of his work it is therefore impossible to overrate. He must be, above all the qualifications of brains and agility usually attributed to that position, of a hopeful or sanguine disposition. He must have confidence in his centre himself, and, most of all, in the man to whom he passes the ball. He should always believe that the play will be a success. The coach can choose no more helpful course during the first few days,

as far as the quarter is concerned, than
that of persuading him to repose confidence in his men. Many promising half-
backs are ruined by the quarter. There
is nothing that makes halves fumble so
badly, get into such awkward positions,
start so slowly, and withal play so half-
heartedly, as the feeling that the quarter
does not think much of them, does not
trust them, or believe in their abilities.
Every half-back can tell the same story
—how he is nerved up by the confidence
of the quarter, and what an inspiration
it is to good work to see that confident
look in the eye of the man who is about
to pass to him. But not alone in the
work of the half does it make a great
difference, but in that of the quarter
himself. When he lacks confidence in
his man, his passing is unsteady and er-
ratic as well as slow. He allows the
opponents a far better chance of reach-

ing the man before he can get started,
both by irregular and slow passing, and
also by a nervous looking at him before
the ball is played.

In practice, great stress should be laid
on quick handling and sharp passing of
the ball. A quarter can slow up in a
game if advisable, but he can never do
any faster work than that which he does
in practice without throwing his men
completely out. In order to make the
play rapid, a quarter must be figuratively
tied to the centre's coat, or rather jacket,
tails. As soon as the centre reaches the
ball after a down, he should know that
the quarter is with him. Usually there
is an understood signal between them,
which not only shows the centre that
the quarter is on hand, but also when he
is ready to receive the ball. One of the
most common of these signals has been
placing the hand upon the centre's leg

or back. A pinch would let him know
when to snap the ball. In spite of this
method's having been used by opponents to fool a centre, it has been, and
still is, the most common. One of the
best variations of it has been for the
quarter to put his hand upon the centre
and keep it there until he is ready for
the ball, then take it off and let the
centre snap the ball, not instantly, but
at his convenience. Should anything
occur making it advisable, for some reason, to stop the play, the quarter puts
his hand upon the centre again at once,
and until it is once more removed the
snap-back understands that the quarter
is not ready to have the ball come. Almost any amount of variation can be
made in the signal of the quarter to his
centre; but in arranging this it should
be constantly borne in mind that the
signal should not be such as to give the

opponents the exact instant of the play, because it gives them too close an idea of the moment when they may start.

The speed of a quarter's work depends upon his ability to take the ball close to the snap-back and in proper position for a pass. In merely handing the ball to a runner, one might suppose that there would be no particular position in which the ball should be held; but in that he would be in error, for a ball so handed to a passing runner as not to settle properly in his arms or hands means in many instances a disastrous fumble, or at best a slowing-up of the runner's speed. In giving the ball to a passing runner, it should be held free and clear of the quarter's body and slightly tilted, so that it can be taken against the body, and without the use of both hands for more than an instant, because the runner may almost imme-

diately have use for his arm in going
into the line. It is impossible to give
in print the exact angle and method of
holding the ball for this purpose, but
practice and the wishes of the runners,
if consulted, will soon show the quarter
just what is meant. When the ball is
to be passed any considerable distance,
it should be taken so that the end is
well placed against the hand of the
quarter, while the ball itself lies against
the forearm, the wrist being bent sharply. This will enable the quarter to send
the ball swiftly and accurately almost
any distance that it may be necessary to
cover. Of course, in many cases the
ball does not actually rest against the
forearm of the quarter; but this is the
best way of conveying the idea of the
proper position of the hand upon the
point of the ball, and by practising in
this way the correct motion for steady

passing is speedily acquired. In receiving the ball, the right hand, or the hand
with which the throw is made, should be
placed upon the end of the ball, while
the other hand stops its progress, and
should be placed as nearly upon the
opposite end of the ball as convenient.
This is the theoretically proper way of
receiving the ball; practically, the handling cannot be as accurately performed
as this would indicate. If, however, the
quarter will in practice be constantly
aiming at receiving the ball so that his
right hand grasps the end just as his
left hand stops the ball, and settles it
securely against his right, he will find
that after a few weeks he can receive
four out of five snap-backs in such a
way as to make any great amount of arranging the ball for his pass, after it is in
his hands, quite unnecessary. After the
preliminary weeks of practice, and when

in a game, he must bear in mind the fact that, in order of importance, his duties are, first, to secure the ball, no matter how; second, to convey it to his own man, no matter whether in good form or not. He must never pass the ball if he has fumbled it, unless he has a perfectly clear field in which to do it. He must always have it down in preference to taking the slightest risk of losing it. Even though he receive it without a fumble, there may be an opening through in that part of the line towards which his pass is to be delivered; and here, again, he should hold the ball for another down rather than take any chance of the opponents intercepting the pass. After letting the ball go, the quarter should follow his pass; in fact, he should be on the run as the ball leaves his hand. No matter whether the ball be caught or fumbled, he is then

ready to lend assistance; whereas if he
stand still after his pass, he is of no use
to the rest of the play. When the play
is a run, he can do excellent work in interfering; and when the play is a kick,
he can take any opponent who gets
through, and thus aid the half in protecting the kicker. In either case, if his
own man muff or fumble he is close at
hand to lend assistance in an emergency, which otherwise might prove most
disastrous. When lining up the quarter
should take a quick glance, not directly
at the player he is to make the recipient
of the ball, but covering the general position of all the men. In doing this he
locates his individual without making it
apparent to the opponents which man
is to receive the ball. Any amount of
disguise may be practised in the way of
taking a last glance at the wrong man,
or calling out to some one who does not

enter into the play. The chief point, nevertheless, is to avoid that tell-tale glance at the right man which is so difficult to omit.

When the opponents have the ball, the quarter makes an extra man in or near the forward line, and, as a rule, he can by his shrewdness make it very uncomfortable for any point in the line which he chooses to assail. No law can govern his tactics in this respect, but he should be a law unto himself, and show by his cleverness that he is more valuable than any man in the line whose position is fixed. One caution only is worth giving to the quarter in this line of play, and that is, to be less free of going forward sharply when the play is evidently to be a run than when a kick is to be attempted. In the latter case, a quarter can always be sent for his best.

THE HALF-BACK AND BACK

WITH the later changes in the rules the province of the three backs becomes of even greater importance than before, and the development of open play puts a still higher premium upon men who can kick and also upon men who have pace.

As the game is at present played, the back is more of a third half-back than a goal-tend, and so should be trained to half-back work. It has been well said that all that one can ask of the best rush line is to hold the ground their half-backs gain; and when one follows carefully the progress of the play, he sees that this is the proper division of the work. The half-backs, then, must be the ground-gainers of the team. Such work calls for dash and fire—that ability to suddenly concentrate all the bodily energy into an effort that must make way through anything. Every one has such half-backs in mind, but unfortunately many of those half-backs who possess this type of character have not the necessary weight and strength to stand the amount of work required. Although a light man be occasionally found who is particularly muscular and wiry, the constant shock of going into a heavy line of forwards usually proves too exhausting for any but those of middle weight before the end of a season be reached. It is not that the work of a single game proves too much for the light-weight half. It is that in both practice and games he is so overmatched by the weight of the forwards whom he must meet that every week finds him less strong than the preceding, until his playing falls off so markedly that the captain or coach is at last convinced that there is something wrong, and the man is replaced by some one else, often too late to bring the substitute up to anything like the mark he might have reached had he been tried earlier in the season. Such thoughts as these will suggest themselves to the experienced coach when at the outset of a season he has placed before him a number of candidates for the position of half-back, among whom very likely there may be two or three men of perhaps one hundred and forty pounds' weight. Likely enough, too, these men may be at that period easily superior to the middle or heavy weights. In such a case the very best advice that can be whispered in the ear of coach or captain is, to make quarters or ends of them, even though it be only substitute quarters and ends. It will leave the way open for the proper cultivation of half-backs better built to stand the wear and tear of a season.

Almost equally to be deprecated is the waste of time often devoted to making half-backs of slow heavy weights. Only a quick man can perform a half-back's duties successfully; and although much can be left to practice, there must be some natural quickness to build upon. Slow men can be improved far more rapidly in the forward line than among the halves. All this regarding the weight of half-backs applies not only to 'varsity teams, but school teams as well, if one will make the proper proportional changes in weight. That is, a 'varsity player will be called upon to face a forward line averaging one hundred and seventy-five or thereabouts, and men of less than one hundred and thirty-five to one hundred and forty are too light to meet that weight. In school teams the rush line will be some twenty pounds lighter, and the halves can therefore be selected from even one-hundred-and-twenty-five-pound men, if well built. In other words, a half-back ought not to face over twenty-five pounds' difference in weight; and the more that difference is reduced, supposing that speed and agility be retained, the more chance there is of turning out a thoroughly successful player. It is worth while to be thus particular upon the point of the early selection of candidates for the position of half-back, because, while no more work is demanded of them in a game than of others of their side, the quality of that work must be more uniformly good. When a half-back has to tackle, he must be as sure as a steel-trap; when a half-back has to catch, he must be a man to be relied upon ; when a half-back is called upon for a kick, it must be no fluke ; and, although no one expects a half-back to always make on his run the five yards, he must be a man who will not be denied when he is called upon for that last yard which will enable his side to retain the ball.

Almost the first thing to be critically noted by the coach is the way in which a half-back takes the ball from his quarter. The case in which he takes it directly from the hands of this player has been already dwelt upon at some length under the head of the quarter's passing ; but when the ball is thrown or passed some little distance, it is just as important that it be properly received. Except when about to kick, the half-back should be moving when he receives the ball, and, more than that, the reception

of it should have no perceptible effect
upon his movements. In other words,
he must take it as easily and as naturally as a batsman in a ball game drops
his bat after he has hit the ball fairly.
No batsman remembers that he has
had the bat in his hands after the ball
has been hit, and yet, when he is at first
base, he has left his bat behind him at
the plate. Thus a football half-back
should so receive the ball as not to
know the exact instant of taking it,
but find that he has it as he comes
up to the line. It will never do for a
coach to suppose that an inexperienced
half can be told that he must take the
ball "without knowing it," but it is
necessary to explain to a half that until
he does take the ball naturally, and
without having to stop and calculate
about it, he can never come properly up
to the line nor get his whole power on

early. To acquire the habit of taking a pass easily, a half-back should spend a little time every day off the field in practising taking a sharp pass when on the run. By a sharp pass is not meant hurling the ball with all possible force against a runner so that he is nearly knocked over by it, and cannot by any possibility catch it except at the expense of giving the catch his sole and undivided attention. Such passing in practice does far more harm than good. The ball should be passed with that easy swing which sends it rapidly, accurately, and evenly up to the runner without any great apparent force, for it is remarkable how much the appearance of force tends to rattle the runner, who easily handles fully as much speed properly delivered. Daily practice of this nature between the quarter and half accustoms each to the other, so that the regular work of the team on the field is not disorganized by loose passing and looser catching. While this passing is progressing, the coach should stand by the side of the half, and watch him closely, correcting any careless tendencies of receiving or stopping, and paying particular attention to his going in a straight line—that is, not running up to meet the ball and then sheering off again. The best half-backs endeavor to receive the ball at approximately the same height relative to their bodies, no matter how it comes, and they will correct quite a variation in the quarter's throw by a little stoop or a slight jump. A half-back must be taught to be uniform in starting, and in reaching the spot where the ball is to meet him. The coach will have no great difficulty in teaching him this steady uniformity of pace, which will enable the quarter to

8

throw the ball so as really to assist rather than retard his motion. There are two other things which the half-back must practise apart from his team-play. They are kicking and catching. The former is of sufficient importance to deserve a separate chapter, but a few hints under the half-back column will not be out of place. There was a time when the running game had so fascinated American captains and coaches, together with their teams, that the great value of long, well-placed kicks was, in a great measure, lost sight of ; but such a state of affairs can no longer prevail, and every team, to be successful in matches with their equals in the other points of the play, should bring out a good method of executing a kicking game when called for. It is usually the case that of all three men behind the line, the two halves and the back, any one can do the kicking upon a pinch, but one of the three is, nine times out of ten, manifestly superior to the other two. In this state of affairs there is altogether too great a tendency to slight the practice of the two inferior kickers, and rely almost entirely upon the best man. It is quite proper to let the best man do all the kicking possible in an important game, but it is a very short-sighted policy to neglect the practice of the other two during the preliminary games. Not only should they have the advantage to be gained in the length of their kicks by daily practice, but they should also have the steadying experience to be acquired only in games. It may happen at any moment in a most important game that the kicking will devolve upon one of them on account of an accident to the third man, and it is, indeed, a foolhardy captain or coach who has not taken suf-

ficient forethought for this contingency.
The principal reason why we develop so
few really good kickers is, that coaches,
captains, and players have given so little attention to the detail of that part
of the work. Fully nine tenths of the
men who do the kicking upon American
teams are more natural kickers than
practised ones. Let me explain this so
as to be fully understood. As in boxing one often sees a man who, having
taken no lessons, and being therefore
unable to make the most of himself,
can yet more than hold his own against
a more finished opponent on account of
his natural quickness, strength, and apti-
tude; so in football one sees here and
there a man who is able to do some fair
kicking without having devoted particular attention to it. In boxing, however,
when a teacher takes the natural hitter
in hand, he begins by putting him at

work upon the rudiments of guarding,
holding himself upon his feet, hitting
straight, and moving firmly.   He never
undertakes to make a first-class man of
him by merely encouraging him to go
in harder, and increase his power without regard to the proper methods.   In
football, coaches rarely teach the kickers the first principles, but instead urge
upon them only the necessity of constant practice in their own way.   For
this reason our kickers show all manner
of styles, and the only wonder is that
they kick so well in such wretchedly
bad form.   One would think that the
increased value placed upon kicking in
the last few years would have corrected
this, but it has only done so in part.
The finished kickers can still be num-
bered upon the fingers of one hand.

While it is neither advisable nor necessary that a kicker be prevented from

attempting to kick hard until he has mastered every detail of the swing and brought it to the same point of perfection that a finished oarsman does his stroke, it certainly is best, in his practice, to subordinate power to method until he acquire good form.

The coach should take his man in hand by watching him make a half-dozen kicks in his own way. Then he should select the worst of his faults, and show him why it is a fault, and how to correct it. He should keep him upon this one point for a few days, until he is convinced that there will be no backsliding, and then begin upon the next. In this way a few weeks will serve to make a second-class man a good one, and open the way for his becoming something out of the ordinary run in another season.

In judging the faults of a kicker, the

coach should note just where he gets
his power on, what is the position of
his leg and foot upon the swing, and
what part of the foot strikes the ball.
These are the principal points, and deserve the first attention. Regarding
the first of these, his power should be
put on just as his foot has passed the
lowest part of the arc in which it swings,
and it should meet the ball in the up-
ward sweep very soon after passing this
point. The position of his leg and foot
is to be next noted, and the " snap
the whip " phrase is as good a one to
convey the idea as any that can be
adopted. As the leg begins to swing
the knee is bent and the body pitched
a little forward, so that the weight of
the kick seems to start from the hip
and travel down the leg as it straight-
ens, reaching the foot just as it meets
the ball, as above mentioned. As for

the third point, the ball, when punted, should be struck by the instep and not by the toe. In a drop-kick and a place-kick the ball is met by the toe, and the sweep is made with "a longer leg," as the expression has it; that is, the foot swings nearer—in fact, almost along the ground.

All these three points can be most clearly illustrated by noting the effect of departures from them. If the power is not put on as above described, the man will simply send the ball along the ground, or will hook it up, merely tossing it with his foot instead of driving it. These two are the extremes, of course; but they illustrate where the power is lost or wasted. If the leg be not swung in proper position, the ball will be simply spatted with the foot, the only force coming from the knee. Finally, if the ball be not met with the proper part of the foot it may snap downwards off the toe, or be merely bunted by the ankle. There is still another thing to be watched, which, while not the kick proper, really belongs to it as much as the swing of the leg. It is the way in which the ball is dropped to the foot from the hand or hands. The usual tendency of beginners, and many half-backs who could hardly be classed in that category, is to toss the ball from the hand ; that is, to give it a motion up from the hand, which, however slight, causes much valuable time to be lost. The ball should always be dropped to the foot, the distance between the hand and foot being made as short as possible. The hand should be merely withdrawn just at the proper moment, and with practice it is not difficult to make the entire transfer from hand to foot so rapid as to almost eliminate any danger of having the ball stopped or struck during

that part of the play. In drop-kicking
the fall is necessarily greater, but it
should never be a toss even then. There
has been no little argument as to whether the ball should be held in one or both
hands by a player about to kick, and such
are the examples of good kickers arrayed
on both sides that we cannot fairly say
that either way is the only right way.
If a player has become so accustomed to
the two-hand method as to make him
uncomfortable and inaccurate if forced
to the one-hand way, it is hardly advisable to make the change. But any
player who is taken early enough can
be taught to drop the ball with one
hand, to his great advantage in both
quickness and ability to kick from tight
quarters or around an opponent.

The entire series of motions, therefore, which go to make up a well-per-
formed kick should be in the coach's

mind just as the separate parts of an oarsman's stroke are in the boating man's mind when coaching a crew. The ball dropped, not tossed; the leg well swung, the power coming from both leg and hip with all the advantage that the poise of the body may add; the foot meeting the ball with the top of the instep on a punt, with the toe on a drop, and in either case just after passing the lowest point of the arc of swing, rather later on a punt than a drop, because the ground helps the latter to rise, while the rise of the former must come entirely from the foot. The next step in the education of the kicker is the side swing. The ball cannot be kicked as far when met directly in front of the kicker—his leg swinging straight, as it would in taking a step in running—as it can be kicked by taking a side sweep with the leg and body, the hips acting as a sort of pivot.

One of the most common false ideas regarding this side-kick is, that it is not performed with the same part of the foot as the straight punt, but that the ball is struck by the side of the foot. Of course, this is all wrong. The foot meets the ball as fairly and directly as it does in the ordinary straight kick, and the ball impinges upon the top of the instep just as before, the word "side" referring to the swing of the leg and position of the body only.

All the suggestions thus far have been applicable to both half-backs and back, but before bringing the chapter to an end it is well to note a few of the special features of the full-back's position. The place originally was that of a goal-tend, but with the increase of the aggressive system of defence his duties have become more those of a third half-back. Other things being equal, it is eminently proper to select as a full-back an exceptionally strong tackler; but as for placing tackling ability above that of kicking, that is a mistake which might have been made six years ago, but of which no coach or captain would to-day be guilty.

The importance of the position is rapidly growing, and under the present rules there is no doubt that the time has come when the selection of the three men behind the line should be after this fashion—namely, picking out the three best half-backs, all things considered, then selecting that one of the three whose kicking is the best, and making him the third half or full back. After the man has been in this way chosen there will devolve upon him certain duties which do not commonly fall to the lot of the other two half-backs. Chiefest among these is the duty of making a running return of a kick, something for which the opportunity seldom offers, but which it is very important that a full-back should be able to do upon occasion. The opponents have sent a punt down towards him, which he secures while the opponents are still some yards away from him, although they are coming down rapidly. In this case, a thoroughly finished player will not only gain a few steps before he takes his kick, but he will take that kick on the run, sometimes dodging the first man before taking the kick. A full-back who can do this and never lose his kick is the greatest kind of a treasure for any team, and it is worth a captain's while to devote a good bit of attention to the full-back's perfecting this special feature of his play.

He will also be likely to have the long place-kicking to do. In fact, it is proper to practise him at this, because, if he be the best punter among the men behind the line, he can be made the longest place-kicker, and few realize the great advantage of these long place-kicks to a team upon occasion of fair catches, especially when a favoring wind brings the possibility of a field-kick goal.

Tackling, when it does fall to the lot of a full-back, comes with an importance the like of which no other player is ever called upon to face. It usually means a touch-down if he misses. For practice of this kind it is well to play the 'varsity back once in a while upon the scrub side. This is likely to improve the speed of his kicking also.

SIGNALS

WHEN Rugby football was first adopted in this country, there was a strong feeling that it would never make progress against what had been known as the American game. This old-fashioned game was much more like the British Association in a rather demoralized state. Not only was there no such thing as offside, but one of the chief features consisted of batting the ball with the fist, at which many became sufficiently expert to drive the ball almost as far as the ordinary punter now kicks it. There was very little division of players by name, although they strung out along the field, and one (known as the "peanutter"—why, no one knows) played in

the enemies' goal. Coming to players
accustomed to this heterogeneous ming-
ling, it is no great wonder that the first
days of Rugby were characterized by
even less system than that displayed in
the old game.

The first division of players was into
rushers, half-backs, and a goal-tend. The
rushers had but little regard for their relative positions in the line; and as for their
duties, one can easily imagine how little
they corresponded with those of the rusher of to-day when it is said that it was
by no means unusual for one of them to
pick up the ball and punt it.

The snap-back and quarter-back play
soon defined these two positions, and
shortly after the individual rush-line positions became distinct, both as regards
location and duties.   All this was an era
of development of general play with but
few particular combinations or marks of

strategy. If a man made a run, he made it for the most part wherever he saw the best chance after receiving the ball, and he made it unaided to any degree by his comrades. If the ball was kicked, it was at the option of the man receiving it, and the forwards did not know whether he would kick or run.

It was at this point that the demand for signals first showed itself. The rushers began to insist upon it that they must be told in some way whether the play was to be a kick or a run. They maintained quite stoutly and correctly that there was no reason in their chasing down the field when the half-backs did not kick. As a matter of fact, the forwards even went so far as to contend that the running-game should be entirely dropped in favor of one based upon long kicks well followed up. Failing to establish this opinion, they nevertheless brought it about that they should be told by some signal what the play was to be, and so be spared useless running. This was probably the first of the present complicated system of signals, although at about the same time some teams took up the play of making a rather unsatisfactory opening for a runner in the line, and made use of a signal to indicate the occasions when this was to be done. The signalling of the quarter to the centre-rush as to when the ball should be played antedated this somewhat, but can hardly be classed with signals for the direction of the play itself.

To-day the teams which meet to decide the championship are brought up to the execution of at least twenty-five different plays (some teams have actually had nearly a hundred), each of which is called for by a certain distinct signal of its own.

The first signals given were "word

signals;" that is, a word or a sentence called out so that the entire team might hear it and understand whether a kick or a run was to be made. Then, when signals became more general, "sign signals" (that is, some motion of the hand or arm to indicate the play) were brought in and became for a time more popular than the word signals, particularly upon fields where the audience pressed close upon the lines, and their enthusiastic cheering at times interfered with hearing word signals. Of late years numerical combinations have become most popular, and as the crowd is kept at such a distance from the side lines as to make it possible for teams to hear those signals, they have proven highly satisfactory. The numerical system, while it can be readily understood by the side giving the signal, because they know the key, is far more difficult for the opponents to solve than either the old word signals or signs. Still, the ingenuity of captains is generally taxed to devise systems that shall so operate as never to confuse their own men and yet completely mystify the opponents throughout the game. Clever forwards almost always succeed in interpreting correctly one or two of the signals most frequently used, in spite of the difficulty apparent in the solution of such problems. The question as to who should give the signals is still a disputed one, although the general opinion is that the quarter-back should perform this duty. There is no question as to the propriety of the signals emanating from that point, but the discussion is as to whether the captain or the quarter should direct the play. Of course all is settled if the captain is himself a quarter-back, but even when he is not he ought to be able to so direct his quarter previous to the actual conflict as to make it perfectly satisfactory to have the signals come from the same place as the ball. It is in that direction that the eyes and attention of every player are more or less turned, and hence signals there given are far more certain to be observed. Moreover, it is sometimes, and by no means infrequently, necessary to change a play even after the signal has been given. This, if the quarter be giving the signals, is not at all difficult, but is decidedly confusing when coming from some other point in the line.

The important fact to be remembered in selecting a system of signals is that it is bad policy to confuse your own team in the attempt to mystify your opponents. A captain must therefore choose such a set of signals as he can be sure of making his own team comprehend without difficulty and without mistake. When he is sure of that, he can think how far it is possible for him to disguise these from his opponents. Among the teams which contest for championship honors it is unusual to find any which are not prepared for emergencies by the possession either of two sets of signals, or of such changes in the manner of giving them as to make it amount to the same thing. Considering the way the game is played at the present time, this preparation is advisable, for one can hardly overestimate the demoralizing effect it would have upon any team to find their opponents in possession of a complete understanding of the signals which were directing the play against them.

While it is well for the captain or coach to arrange in his own mind early in the season such a basis for a code of

signals as to render it adaptable to almost indefinite increase in the number
of plays, it is by no means necessary to
have the team at the outset understand
this basis. In fact, it is just as well to
start them off very modestly upon two
or three signals which they should learn,
and of which they should make use until the captain sees fit to advance them
a peg.

If, for instance, the captain decides
to make use of a numerical system,
he cannot do better to accustom his
men to listening and following instructions than to give them three signals,
something like this: One-two-three, to
indicate that the ball is to be passed to
the right half-back, who will endeavor to
run around the left end; four-five-six,
that the left half will try to run around
the right end; and seven-eight-nine,
that the back will kick. The scrub side

will probably "get on" to these signals in short order, and will make it pleasant at the ends for the half-backs; but this will be the best kind of practice in team work, and will do no harm. After a day or two of this it will be time to make changes in the combination of numbers, not only with an idea of deceiving the scrub side, but also to quicken the wits of the 'Varsity team. Taking the same signals as a basis, the first, or signal for the right half-back to try on the left end, was one-two-three—the sum of these numbers is six. Take that, then, as the key to this signal, and any numbers the sum of which equals six will be a signal for this play. For instance, three-three, or four-two, two-three-one—any of these would serve to designate this play. Similarly, as the signal for the left half at the right end was four-five-six, or a total of fifteen, any

numbers which added make fifteen—
as six-six-three, seven-eight, or five-four-
six—would be interpreted in this way.
Finally, the signal for a kick having
been seven-eight-nine, or a sum of
twenty-four, any numbers aggregating
that total would answer equally well.

A few days of this practice will fit the
men for any further developments upon
the same lines, and accustom them to
listening and thinking at the same time.
The greatest difficulty experienced by
both captains and coaches since the signals and plays became so complicated
has been to teach green players not to
stop playing while they listen to and
think out a signal. By the end of the
season players are so accustomed to
the signals that all this hesitation dis-
appears, and the signal is so familiar as
to amount to a description of the play
in so many words.

The other two methods of signalling by the use of words rather than numbers, and signs given by certain movements, although they have now given way in most teams to numbers, are still made use of, and have merit enough to deserve a line or two. The word-signal was usually given in the form of a sentence, the whole or any part of which would indicate the play. As, for instance, to indicate a kick, the sentence "Play up sharp, Charlie." If the quarter, or who-ever gave the signals, should call out, "Play up," or "Play up sharp," or "Play," or "Charlie," he would in each instance be giving the signal for a kick. Sign-signals are more difficult to dis-guise, but are none the less very effec-tive, especially where there is a great amount of noise close to the ropes. A good example of the sign-signal is the touching of some part of the body with

the hand. For instance, half-back running would be denoted by placing the
hand on the hip, the right hip for the
left half, and the left hip for the right
half. A kick would be indicated by
placing the hand upon the neck. Particular care should be exercised when
sign-signals are to be used that the ones
selected, while similar to the acts performed naturally by the quarter in
stooping over to receive the ball, are
never exactly identical with these motions, else there will likely enough be
confusion.

No matter what method of signalling
be used, there is one important feature
to be regarded, and that is, some means
of altering the play after a signal has
been given. This is, of course, a very
simple thing, and the usual plan is to
have some word which means that the
signal already given is to be considered

void, and a new signal will be given in its place. There should also be some way of advising the team of a change from one set of signals to another, should such a move become necessary. It is very unwise not to be prepared for such an emergency, because if a captain is obliged to have time called and personally advise his team one by one of such a change, the opponents are quite sure to see it and to gain confidence from the fact that they have been clever enough to make such a move necessary.

TRAINING

AT the present advanced athletic era there are very few who do not understand that a certain amount of preparation is absolutely essential to success in any physical effort requiring strength and endurance. The matter of detail is, however, not faced until one actually becomes a captain or a coach, and, as such, responsible for the condition, not of himself alone, but of a team of fifteen or twenty men.

Experience regarding his own needs will have taught him the value of care and work in this line; but, unless he differ greatly from the ordinary captain upon first assuming the duties of that position, his knowledge of training will be confined to an understanding of his own requirements, coupled with the handed-down traditions of the preceding captains and teams. When he finds himself in this position and considers what lines of training he shall lay down for his team, unless he be an inordinately conceited man he will wish he had made more of a study of this art of preparation, especially in the direction most suited to the requirements of his own particular sport.

Many inquiries from men about to undertake the training of a team have led me to believe that, even at the expense of going over old ground, it will be well in this book to map out a few of the important features of a course of training. It should go without saying that there are infinite variations in systems of this kind; but if a man will carry in mind the reasons rather than the rules, he has always a test to apply which will enable him to make the most of whatever system he adopts.

He should remember that training ought to be a preparation by means of which his men will at a certain time arrive at the best limits of their muscular strength and activity, at the same time preserving that equilibrium most conducive to normal health. Such a preparation can be accomplished by the judicious use of the ordinary agents of well-being — exercise, diet, sleep, and cleanliness.

One can follow out the reasons for or against any particular point in a system rather better if he cares to see why these agents act towards health and strength.

Exercise is a prime requisite, because the human mechanism, unlike the inanimate machine, gains strength from use. Muscular movement causes disintegration and death of substance, but at the same time there is an increased flow of blood to the part, and that means an increased supply of nourishment and increased activity in rebuilding. As Mac-Laren has expressed it, strength means newness of the muscle. The amount and quality of this exercise will be treated of later in this chapter.

In considering the matter of Diet, a captain or coach should think of this question not according to the tradition of his club, nor according to his own idiosyncrasies. He should regard the general principle of not depriving a man of anything to which he is accustomed and which agrees with him. Of course, it is advisable to do without such articles of food as would be injurious to the majority of the men, even though there might be one or two to whom they would do no harm. Men should enjoy

their food, and it should be properly
served. I remember once being asked
my opinion regarding a certain team
at the time in training, and I expressed
the conviction that something was
wrong with their diet. The team, as a
whole, were not seriously affected, but
some three or four were manifestly out
of sorts. I heard the coach go over the
bill of fare, and it sounded all right. I
then decided to take dinner with them
and see if I could discover the trouble.
One meal was sufficient, for it was a
meal! The beef — and an excellent
roast it was, too—was literally served in
junks, such as one might throw to a dog.
The dishes were dirty, so was the cloth.
Vegetables were dumped on to the
plates in a mess, and each one grabbed
for what he wanted. Some of the men
might have been brought up to eat at
such a table, still others were not suffi-

ciently sensitive to have their appetites greatly impaired by anything, but the three or four who were " off " were boys whose home life had accustomed them to a different way of dining, and their natures revolted. So, too, did their appetites. As it was then too late to correct the manners of the mess, I simply advised sending these men elsewhere to board, and they speedily came into shape. I cannot too strongly advocate good service at a training table. The men should enjoy their dinners, should eat them slowly, and should be encouraged to be as long about it as they will. As food is to repair the waste, it should be generous in quantity and taken when the man will not, from being over-tired, have lost his appetite. Sometimes a team is not overworked, but worked too late in the day, so that the men rush to the table almost directly from the field, and fail to feel hungry, while within an hour they would have eaten with a zest. This course persevered in for several days will show its folly in a general falling-off in the strength as well as the weight of the men. To train a football team should be, in the matter of the diet at least, the simplest matter compared with training for other sports, because the season of the year is so favorable to good condition.

Crews and ball nines have oftentimes the trial of exceptionally hot and exhausting weather to face, while a football team, after the few warm days of September are passed, enjoy the very best of bracing weather—weather which will give almost any man who spends his time in out-door work a healthy, hearty appetite. In order that any captain or coach reading this book may feel that, while it offers several courses of diet, it would emphatically present the fact that there is no hard-and-fast system of diet that must be religiously followed, I submit a variety of tables, showing some old as well as new school diets. None of them are very bad, several are excellent; and I don't think that a captain or coach would be called upon to draw his pencil through very many of the items enumerated.

THE OXFORD SYSTEM.—(Summer Races.)

A DAY'S TRAINING.*

Rise about 7 A.M.	{ So as to be in chapel; but early rising not compulsory.
Exercise	A short walk or run......Not compulsory (walk only, and short).
Breakfast, 8.30	{ Meat, beef or mutton. { Bread or toast, dry......The crust only recommended. { Tea......As little as possible recommended.
Exercise (forenoon)	{ None......{ American football men should kick, catch, and pass.
Dinner, 2 P.M.	{ Meat; much the same as for breakfast. { Bread......Crust only recommended. { Vegetables, none allowed..A rule, however, not always adhered to. { Beer, one pint......{ This is what Americans call ale, and not indulged in to any great extent except after a hard game.
Exercise	{ About 5 o'clock start for the river, and row twice over the course, the speed increasing with the strength of the crew.
Supper, 8.30 or 9..	{ Meat, cold. { Bread; perhaps a jelly or watercresses. { Beer, one pint (see above).
Bed about 10.	

*As has been stated elsewhere, improvements have been made in diet since this table was compiled. This will also apply to the Cambridge System, page 143.

155

TORPID RACES.

A DAY'S TRAINING.

Rise about 7.30 A.M. . . . . Early rising not compulsory.

Exercise . . . . A short walk or run . . . . Not compulsory.

Breakfast, 9 . . . . As for summer races.

Exercise (forenoon) . . . . . None.

Luncheon about 1 P.M. $\left\{ \begin{array}{l} \text{Bread, or a sandwich.} \\ \text{Beer, half a pint.} \end{array} \right.$

Exercise . . . . $\left\{ \begin{array}{l} \text{About 2 o'clock start for the river,} \\ \text{and row twice over the course.} \end{array} \right.$

Dinner, 5 . . . . $\left\{ \begin{array}{l} \text{Meat, as for summer races.} \\ \text{Bread.} \\ \text{Vegetables, as for summer races.} \\ \text{Pudding (rice), or jelly.} \\ \text{Beer, half a pint.} \end{array} \right.$

Bed, 10.30.

THE CAMBRIDGE SYSTEM. Summer Races (1866).

A DAY'S TRAINING.

Rise at 7 A.M.

Exercise............ { Run 100 or 200 yards as fast as possible. } "The old system of running a mile or so before breakfast is fast going out, except in the case of men who want to get a good deal of flesh off."

Breakfast, 8.30..... { Meat, beef or mutton. Toast, dry. Tea, two cups, or towards the end of a training a cup and a half only. Watercresses occasionally.

Exercise (forenoon)..None.

Dinner about 2 P.M. { Meat, beef or mutton. Bread. Vegetables—potatoes, greens } { Some colleges have baked apples, or jellies, or rice puddings. } Beer, one pint. Dessert — oranges, or biscuits, or figs; wine, two glasses.

Exercise............ { About 5.30 start for the river, and row to the starting-post and back........... } "Most men get out for a little time before rowing back."

Supper about 8.30 or 9. { Meat, cold. Bread. Vegetables—lettuce or watercresses. Beer, one pint.

Bed at 10.

157

H. CLASPER'S SYSTEM.

A DAY'S TRAINING.

Rise between 6 and 7 A.M.

Exercise........A country walk of four or five miles.

Breakfast, 8....
- Meat, chop or
- Couple of eggs.
- Bread.
- Tea. ("We never drink coffee.")

Exercise......Rest for half an hour, and then a brisk walk or run. If morning exercise has not been heavy, a row on the river, terminating about 11 A.M.

Dinner, 12 M..
- Meat, beef or mutton (broiled).
- Egg pudding, with currants in it if desired, or other light farinaceous pudding.
- Ale, one glass.
- Wine, one glass (port), or
- Ale, two glasses, without wine.

Exercise......Rest for an hour, and then on the river again for a hard row. "Rowing exercise should be taken twice every day."

Tea...........
- "Tea, with toasted bread sparingly buttered, with one egg only—more has a tendency to choke the system."

Supper.......Not recommended. When taken, to consist of new milk and bread, or gruel, with raisins and currants and a glass of port wine in it.

Bed about 10.

158

C. WESTHALL'S SYSTEM. For Amateurs.

A DAY'S TRAINING.

Rise at 6 A.M., or earlier in the summer. } Cold bath and rub-down.

Exercise.............. { Sharp walk about a mile out, and run home; or a row of a couple of miles at three-parts speed.
A dry rub-down.

Breakfast (time not stated).... { Meat, mutton-chop or steak (broiled).
Bread, stale or toast.
Tea, half a pint.
(Not stated.)

Exercise............. {

Dinner, 2 P.M............. { Meat (as at breakfast).
Vegetables, none; "except a mealy potato."
Bread, stale.
Beer, one pint.

Exercise (afternoon)............. Rowing.

If dinner be late, luncheon to be taken to consist of Meat, beef or mutton, hot or cold. Bread. Beer, one glass.
(If dinner be early, "tea with viands and liquids as at breakfast" to be taken.)

Supper............. Half a pint of thin gruel, or dry toast and a glass of ale.
Bed............. Time not stated.

N.B.—It is added "that the above rules are of course open to alteration according to circumstances, and the diet varied successfully by the introduction of fowls, either roast or boiled—the latter preferred;" and "it must never be lost sight of that sharp work, regularity, and cleanliness are the chief if not the only rules to be followed to produce thorough good condition."

McLAREN'S SYSTEM.

A DAY'S TRAINING.

Rise at about 7 A.M..(Glass of cold water recommended.)

Exercise..........{ The crew meet at 7, walk and run for four or five miles; or, in later practice, quick run of two miles. Wash and dress.

Breakfast, 9.........{ Meat (broiled); bread (brown) and butter; tea, two cups. "Cocoa made of the nibs boiled for four hours is better than tea for breakfast."
Smoking allowed (conditionally). "Smoking is barred, for, though here also a man's habits are to be taken into account, the subjects of training in match-boats are usually too young to have contracted a custom of smoking so inveterate as to have made tobacco indispensable to the body's internal functions, though it is not unfrequently so in older men. After breakfast is the only time allotted to the pipe."

Luncheon at 1.....{ Beef sandwich with half a pint of beer, or Biscuit and glass of sherry, or egg in sherry.

Exercise..........{ At 2.30 go out to row, and row over the whole course. "This altogether depends on the state of the crew." Wash in tepid water.

McLAREN'S SYSTEM—*Continued.*

Dinner at 6 P.M. ....

Meat (roast, broiled, or boiled). "Any kind of wholesome meat thoroughly cooked."

Vegetables—"The green foods permissible contain in their list spinach—the very best of all; sea-kale, asparagus, but without melted butter; turnip-tops, young unhearted greens, but not solid cabbages; broccoli, carrots, parsnips, and cooked celery. Turnips are also favored, and pease condemned; also cucumbers, and all salad mixtures. But boiled beet-root is good, and Jerusalem artichokes; and French beans stand next to spinach in virtue." The course is varied daily, so that no two days together shall see the same articles on the table.

Pudding. ("Light puddings may be eaten.")

Bread. Beer, one pint.

Wine, two glasses of old port or sherry, or three of claret.

Biscuits and dried fruits, as cherries, figs, etc., allowed. ("All fresh fruits are avoided.")

Jellies. ("Plain jellies are innocuous.")

Water. ("As much spring water as they have a mind to.")

Supper, 9.............Oatmeal gruel if desired.
Bed at 10.

N. B.—On Sundays a brisk walk of three hours or so is taken.

SUMMARY.

Sleep, eight or nine hours.   Exercise, about three hours.   Diet, very varied.

STONEHENGE'S SYSTEM.

A DAY'S TRAINING.

Rise at 8 A.M. ..... { According to season and weather. Cold bath.

Exercise, 8.30 to 9... Walking or running. "Let all take a gentle run or smart walk."

Breakfast, 9 to 9.30 { Oatmeal porridge, with meat (beef or mutton, broiled) and bread. Tea or coffee, or table beer, one pint. "Tea is preferred to coffee. Cocoa is too greasy."

Exercise, 9.30 to 11.30, Billiards, skittles, quoits, or other light exercise.

11.30 to 1.30...... Rowing.

1.30 to about { Running. "According to circumstances." Rubbed dry and linen changed.
2.30.

Dinner, 2.30 to 3 { Meat—beef (roast) or mutton (boiled mutton occasionally), roast fowl, partridges, or pheasants (allowed), or venison (nothing better). "It is generally directed that the steak or chop should be under-done; this, I am sure, is a fallacy."—Bread (*ad lib.*).—Puddings occasionally, made of bread, eggs, and milk, and served with pre-served fruits.—Vegetables—potatoes (one or two only), cauliflow-ers, and broccoli (only as an occasional change). If training is pro-tracted, fish allowed (cod or soles).—Beer, from a pint to a pint and a half.—Wine, a glass or two, port or sherry.

After dinner, until 5 or 6..A gentle stroll or book.

Exercise, 6 to 7...... Rowing.

Supper, 8 .... Oatmeal porridge with dry toast or chop, with glass of port.

Bed at 9 or 10.

BREAKFAST.—Stale or whole-meal bread, or toast, a little butter, plenty of marmalade if you like, but not jam. Bacon and eggs, or chops or steaks, with watercress if obtainable. To those who like it, a basin of oatmeal porridge, *properly made*, taken with pure milk about an hour before breakfast, is an excellent thing, and has a very beneficial effect upon the stomach, but it should not be taken every day. It is better to miss it every third day, or to take it regularly for a fortnight and then omit it from the next week's diet, as the too frequent use of it is rather injurious to the skin of some persons. Tea—not too strong—is better than coffee. Good ripe fruit is a capital adjunct to the breakfast-table, and is an excellent article of food.

DINNER.—Lamb, mutton, beef, fowl (tender and boiled), varied by fish, of which haddock, whiting, and soles are the best, with potatoes (well boiled, and not much of them), and well-cooked vegetables, followed by a small allowance of light farinaceous pudding or stewed fruit, will be a good, wholesome diet. If you want bread, have it stale. Never eat *new* bread. Avoid all sauces, or made dishes, and adhere to plain food only. One thing we would particularly impress upon the reader, and that is never to take his exercise immediately before or after meals, nothing is more injurious, or likely to produce indigestion, and its concomitant evils. Some authorities abjure the use of sugar, but taken in moderation it is not injurious. A well-known champion of our acquaintance, when in the pink of condition, was wont to amuse himself by eating the contents of a sugar basin, if one were inadvertently left near him, and without feeling any ill effects from so doing. Our readers need not follow his example, for although it might suit him, it probably would not agree with them. We have said, take sugar in *moderation*. Now, in this last word lies all the lectures one can give on this subject. Be moderate in all things, one might say, but above all things be moderate in the use of all edibles not actually necessary to support the increased exertion which a man in training is called upon to perform. No liquid should be taken except with, or just after meals, but we would not advise stinting the quantity too much. In summer three or four pints, and in winter two or three pints per diem would be about the quantity. Never drink just before exercise, and it is better not to drink just before going to bed. In fact, the less one has to digest when retiring for sleep the better, and be sure not to drink tea late at night.

TEA, or SUPPER, should be taken at least two hours before bedtime, and we would allow a small chop, or some light fish, bread, and very little butter, with some ripe fruit. The best meal to take before a race, and which should be taken about two hours before starting-time, is the lean of mutton-chops and a little dry toast. We have said that no liquids should be taken except at meal-times; but we do not intend to state that if a man be very thirsty he may not touch them. If he does so, it must be a very small quantity. Thirst can often be assuaged by rinsing the mouth out with cold water, and this is by far the better plan if it is efficacious.

A COMMON-SENSE SYSTEM

ONE author says: "Rise at six; bathe; take about two ounces (a small cup) of coffee with milk: this is really a stimulating soup. Then light exercise, chiefly devoted to lungs; a little rest; the breakfast of meat, bread, or oatmeal, vegetables, with no coffee; an hour's rest. Then the heaviest exercise of the day. This is contrary to rule; but I believe the heaviest exercise should be taken before the heaviest meal; a rest before dinner. This meal, if breakfast be taken at seven or eight, should be at one or two, not leaving a longer interval than five hours between the meals. At dinner, again meat, vegetables, bread, perhaps a half - pint of malt liquor, no sweets. Then a longer rest; exercise till five. Supper light — bread, milk, perhaps with an egg. Half an hour later a cup of tea, and bed at nine."

SEVEN o'clock is a good time for an athlete in training to rise. He ought to get a good dry-rubbing, and then sponge his body with cold water, or have a shower-bath, with a thorough rubbing afterwards. He will then go out to exercise before breakfast, not to run hard, as is commonly taught, but to walk briskly for an hour, while exercising his lungs in deep-breathing. Before this walk, an egg in a cup of tea, or something of the kind, should be taken.

The breakfast need not always consist of a broiled mutton-chop or cutlet; a broiled steak, broiled chicken, or broiled fish, or some of each, may be taken with tea or coffee.

Dinner may be far more varied than is usually allowed by the trainer's "system." Any kind of butcher's meat, plainly cooked, with a variety of fresh vegetables, may be taken, with ordinary light puddings, stewed fruit, but no pastry. A good time for dinner is one o'clock.

An American athlete, when thirsty, ought to have only one drink—water. The climate and the custom in England favor the drinking of beer or claret; but, beyond question, the best drink for a man in training is pure water. After dinner, rest, but no dozing or *siesta*. This sort of rest only spoils digestion, and makes men feel slack and "limp."

Supper, at six o'clock, should not be a second dinner; but neither should it consist of "slops" or gruel. The athlete ought to be in bed by ten o'clock, in a room with open window, and a draught through the room, if possible, though not across the bed.

The American football captain or coach should bear in mind, when reading these various systems, that the use of ale and port seems to be much better borne by those who live in the English climate than upon this side the water.

Also, that stiff exercise before breakfast has not been proven advantageous to our athletes except as a flesh-reducer, and then only in exceptionally vigorous constitutions.

Also, that tea is not as popular with us as with the men who train in England.

SLEEP AND CLEANLINESS

To come to the third agent of health enumerated some pages back, Sleep. As a rule, it is not a difficult matter to see that members of a football team take the requisite amount of sleep. There are occasions, as in college, when some society event of unusual importance tempts the men to sit up late, but with such exceptions as these there is no great difficulty experienced in making the majority of the men keep good hours. And this is growing more and more simple as athletics become more general, for they take the place of much of the dissipation which was formerly the only outlet for the superabundant animal spirits of young men. In the case, however, of the occasional candidate for the team who comes under the captain's eye as inclined to late hours, there must be the strictest kind of discipline shown. Such a man is the very one whose stamina will be affected after a while by lack of sleep, and that too at a time when the rest of the men are nearing the perfection of condition. Thus he will be found falling off at the very time when it is a most serious matter very likely to fill his position with a new man. Eight or nine hours sleep should be insisted upon, and that sleep should be taken with regularity. In fact, not only the sleep, but the meals and the exercise, should all be made as nearly regular, regarding hours, as possible. Men should have separate rooms, and particularly when off upon trips they should not sleep together. Plenty of fresh air should be admitted to the sleeping-room, but draughts are to be avoided. This is not because every time the air blows upon a man he is liable to contract a severe cold, for the chances are against this, but because there are times when he is particularly prone to such an accident, and if he is in the habit of sleeping without regard to draughts it is not likely that he will take precautions then. If a man has, for instance, played an especially stiff game and upon a muggy and exhausting day, he will undoubtedly turn in thoroughly tired out, and perhaps still somewhat heated. Now if he, when in that state, sleeps in a draught, he will probably find himself very lame in the morning, even though he escape other more serious consequences. Just one more word of caution regarding sleep, and that is in the matter of obtaining a good night's rest just before the important match of the season. To insure this is to do much towards securing the best work of which the men are capable from the team upon the following day.

First and foremost, they should not be allowed to talk about the game or the signals or anything connected with football during that evening. If possible, they should do something to entirely divert their minds from all thought of the game. Nor should they be hustled off to bed an hour or two earlier than usual. Rather ought it to be a half-hour later, for then the chances are that the men drop off to sleep immediately instead of tossing about, thinking of the exciting event of the morrow.

Finally, as to overtrained men, and that restlessness and inability to sleep that almost always comes with the worst cases of this kind. There is but one thing to do with a man when he "goes fine" to this extent, and that is to sever his connection with the team for a time. If it is early in the season, there is some chance of his recuperating rapidly enough to still become serviceable. If it is late, there is no hope of this. In either case he must neither play, eat, nor spend his time with the members of the team. He can do almost anything else; he can go and watch the crew row or the ball nine play; he can study or read; he can, and in fact should, do everything possible to disassociate himself from football and violent exercise for a time, and, unless the trouble has gone too far, it will only be a couple of weeks before he will find himself coming out of it all right, and among the first signs will be good, refreshing sleep.

To pass now to the fourth of our agents for health, Cleanliness. It is fort-

unately seldom necessary to argue the
advantages of the "tub" or "sponge
bath" to our football players, because
they are usually accustomed to it. A
daily splashing has been their ordinary
habit. It is well to mention also that a
fortnightly warm bath may be indulged
in to advantage. But with the present
understanding of all these advantages,
the wisest remarks that can be made
are cautions as to indiscretions in the
use of baths. In the first place, one
bath a day is enough, and any other
should be a mere sponging and rubbing. Men who indulge in a tub in
the morning and then spend another
fifteen minutes in a plunge after practice in the afternoon get too much of it.
Again, the habit of spending a long time
under the shower every day is a mistake. It feels so refreshing after a hard
practice that a man is tempted to stay

12

too long, and it does him no good. The best and safest plan is to take a light, quick sponge bath in the morning immediately upon rising, and then, after practice in the afternoon, to take just a moment under the shower, and follow it by a good rubbing. This, with the fortnightly warm bath, will be all that a man may do to advantage.

A CHAPTER FOR SPECTATORS

To those who have never played the game of football, but who chance to open the covers of this book, a short explanation of the divisions and duties of the players will not be out of place. For these this chapter is added.

The game is played by two teams, of eleven men each, upon a field 330 feet long and 160 feet wide, at either end of which are goal-posts with a cross-bar.

The ball, which is like a large leather egg, is placed in the centre of this field, and each team endeavors to drive it in the direction of the opponents' goal-line, where any scoring must be done. Goals and touch-downs are the only points which count, and these can be made only as follows:

A goal can be obtained by kicking the ball in any way except a punt (a certain kind of kick where the ball is dropped by a player and kicked before touching the ground) over the cross-bar of the opponents' goal. A touch-down is obtained by touching the ball to the ground behind the line of the goal. So, in either case, the ball must cross the end of the field in some way to make any score. The sole object, then, of all the struggles which take place in the field is to advance the ball to a position such that scoring is possible. A firm grasp of this idea usually simplifies matters very much for the casual spectator.

The object of the white lines which cross the field at every five yards is merely to assist the referee in determining how far the ball moves at a time; for there is a rule which states that a team must advance the ball five yards

in three attempts or retreat with it
twenty. If they do not succeed in doing this, the other side take possession
of the ball, and in their turn try to advance it.

There are certain rules which govern
the methods of making these advances,
any infringement of which constitutes
what is called *a foul*, and entails a penalty upon the side making it.

Any player can run with the ball or
kick it if, when he receives it, he is " on
side "—that is, between the ball and his
own goal-line. He may not take the
ball if he is "off side" — that is, between the ball and his opponents' goal-
line — until an adversary has touched
the ball.

Whenever a player running with the
ball is held, the referee blows his whistle,
and a man of his side then places the ball
on the ground and snaps it back.   This

puts it in play, and is called a scrimmage, and this scrimmage is the most commonly recurring features of the game.

For the purposes of advancing the ball or repelling the attack of the opponents it has proved advisable for a captain to divide his eleven men into two general divisions : the forwards and backs. The forwards, of whom there are seven, are usually called rushers, and five at least of them make practically a straight line across the field when the ball is put in play on a "down." Next behind them is the quarter-back, who does the passing of the ball to one or another of the players, while just behind him are the two half-backs and the back, with often near them two men properly of the rush line.

The following definitions will also aid the spectator in understanding many of the expressions used by the devotees of the sport:

A *drop-kick* is made by letting the ball fall from the hands, and kicking it at the very instant it rises from the ground.

A *place-kick* is made by kicking the ball after it has been placed on the ground.

A *punt* is made by letting the ball fall from the hands, and kicking it before it touches the ground.

Kick-off is a place-kick from the centre of the field of play.

Kick-out is a drop - kick, place - kick, or punt, by a player of the side which has touched the ball down in their own goal, or into whose touch-in-goal the ball has gone.

In touch means out of bounds.

A *fair* is putting the ball in play, from touch.

A *foul* is any violation of a rule.

A *touch-down* is made when the ball is carried, kicked, or passed across the goal-line and there held, either in goal or touch-in-goal.

A *safety touch-down* is made when a player, guarding his goal, receives the ball from a player of his own side, and touches it down behind his goal-line, or carries the ball across his own goal-line and touches it down, or puts the ball into his own touch-in-goal.

A *touch-back* is made when a player touches the ball to the ground behind his own goal, the impetus which sent the ball across the line having been received from an opponent.

A *fair catch* is a catch made direct from a kick by one of the opponents, provided the catcher make a mark with his heel at the spot where he made the catch.

Foul interference is using the hands or arms in any way to obstruct or hold a player who has not the ball.

The *penalty* for fouls and violation of rules, except otherwise provided, is a down for the other side; or, if the side making the foul has not the ball, ten yards to the opponents.

The following is the value of each point in the scoring :

Goal obtained by touch-down,   .   6

Goal from field kick, ...   5

Touch-down failing goal, .   .   .   4

Safety by opponents, ...   2

The rules which bear most directly upon the play are :

The time of a game is seventy minutes, each side playing thirty-five minutes from each goal.   There is ten minutes' intermission between the two halves, and the game is decided by the score of even halves.

The ball is kicked off at the beginning of each half; and whenever a goal has been obtained, the side which has lost it kicks off.

A player may throw or pass the ball in any direction except towards opponents' goal. If the ball be batted or thrown forward, it shall go down on the spot to opponents.

If a player having the ball be tackled and the ball fairly held, the referee blows his whistle and some player of the side having the ball puts it down for a scrimmage. If, in three consecutive fairs and downs, unless the ball cross the goal-line, a team shall not have advanced the ball five or taken it back twenty yards, it shall go to the opponents on the spot of the fourth down.

If the ball goes into touch, whether it bounds back or not, a player on the side which touches it down must bring it to the spot where the line was crossed, and there either touch the ball in the field of play, with both hands, at right angles to the touch-line, and then kick it, or walk out with it at right angles to touch-line, any distance not less than five nor more than fifteen yards, and there put it down for a scrimmage.

A side which has made a touch-down in their opponents' goal *must* try at goal.

When the ball is put in play in a scrimmage five men must be on the line of scrimmage.

Five players, not including the quarter-back, may be behind the line of scrimmage, provided two at least be either five yards back or outside the positions occupied by the players on the end of the line.

Only one man of the side putting the ball in play may be in motion, and he only in the direction of his own goal.

INTERFERENCE AND WEDGE PLAY

SINCE adding to the second edition of this book an appendix upon Team Play, in which I commented at some length upon that play known as the Wedge, as well as Interference, the progress in development of both these plays, and the fortunate opportunity offered by the publication of a third edition, tempts me to add a chapter upon the further advance upon these lines. To thoroughly understand Interference in American football, one must go step by step along the line which our players have followed both in legislation and in practical development upon the field of play.

The chief factor of modern football

is team play, and the point towards which team play is principally directed is the interference for the runner. The growth of interference was at first a peculiar one, for, as a matter of fact, it was illegal, and so recognized by captains, players, and judges. But for all that, the temptation to indulge in it was so great and the liability to discovery so small that line-men made use of it with what was coming to be alarming frequency. The rule was flat in its statement that a man when off side could not interrupt or obstruct an opponent unless he had the ball. There could be no mincing matters about this, for any man who was ahead of the runner was off side, and hence must not interrupt or obstruct the opponent. The trouble began in the rush-line when drawn up for a down. Of course they could not, when the ball was snapped back behind them, help being off side, and no more could they avoid being an interruption and obstruction to their opponents unless they melted at once into thin air. They therefore stood their ground. Then they went further: they extended their arms from their sides, thus making it very difficult to get through their ranks. But for a time that was the limit of their offence. Gradually, however, those arms took to hooking themselves too closely about a man who was near the runner, and before long they were actually dragging him out of the runner's path. Up to this time there was almost no interference in the open—it was all in the line. But it became impossible for the umpire to stop the practice entirely, because he could not draw the line between what must be allowed and what should be stopped. If he ruled liter-

ally that no man, when the ball was
snapped behind him, could interrupt or
obstruct an adversary, what could he
do with the whole forward line? Make
them move off the field, or forbid the
centre to snap the ball? The wisest
course of all seemed to be to face the
situation fairly, admit that a certain
amount of interference was unavoida-
ble, but place limits to that interference
which should be clear and thoroughly
understood by player and umpire. This
method was adopted, and rules so altered as to make it fair for a man who
was off side to interrupt or obstruct the
would-be tacklers of the other side, provided that in doing it he did not make
use of his hands or arms. Primarily,
this rule at once brought down to their
sides the arms of the forwards in the
line on a down. In fact, it was upon
this point that a great deal of the dis-

cussion prior to the passage of the rule
depended. It was even argued by one
of the opponents of the measure that
forwards could not protect themselves
from injury at the hands of the charging adversaries unless they were allowed to extend their arms and thus
push them off. But with all the opposition, the measure went through, and
from it has grown one of the most scientific features of the play. Perhaps
the simplest form of interference was in
the tandem play, where a single man
would precede the runner, and by charging through the line, make an opening
for him to follow, at the same time dis-
tracting the attention of those about to
tackle from the man with the ball.

As a matter of fact, there is now almost no play in the game into which
good interference may not find an entry.
So it comes about that one of the im-

portant attributes of the modern coach is an ability to adapt all the plays of his team to the amount of interference of which they are capable. He may have strong and agile guards, whose weight is not so great as to preclude the possibility of their getting into the interfering line of almost every play. He may have some very valuable but light man, who can be used only to a limited extent against heavy opponents if he is to be kept fresh for his own individual work. It is no uncommon mistake made by captains at present to thus exhaust a light, dashing man, by using him too injudiciously in heavy interference, thereby rendering him unfit for special work. Of course every coach and captain knows better than to put a small quarter up into the peak of a wedge, to be smashed into disability by the charging heavy weights of the opponents, but there are other places where his interference is none the less hazardous. This really is the first point to be considered in laying out the interference of a team—to so use the men as to leave them still in condition to perform their own special parts of the regular work. The coach should apply this to every plan for interference, making it a test question before proceeding to develop the play.

To begin with the opening play so common formerly among all teams, the close wedge. In this play almost the entire team were used as interferers, the runner and the two or three lightest men being the ones who went inside. Although this play has now been replaced by a kick, there are still many plays directed at the centre or guards which partake very closely of the original wedge formation, only differing in the number of men involved and the time of the formation. Then there are the plays directed at the tackle, where the run is short and straight forward. Here the two men making the opening are the chief interferers, and they select their men and crowd them apart just as the runner plunges forward into the opening. It is the custom to combine this with the tandem system, running one or even two men through this opening in advance of the man with the ball, and still another man behind him to push. In the event of one or more of the men preceding the runner succeeding in getting through and clear of the line, they are expected to make themselves useful by proceeding down the field and interfering with the halves and back. The run around by the tackle involves a similar method of interference, his opening being made in precisely the same manner as the opening for a running half or back.

But it is in plays around the end or between the end and the tackle that interference is developed in its highest form. Here it is not a question of quickly separating two men for a moment, until a runner can plunge between them and then shift for himself. It is rather a prolonged and continuous blocking off of, it may be, seven or eight men, and some of these not only once, but two or three times in the course of the play, while the runner circles around behind this line of protectors, until, if the play be properly made, he comes flying by the end of that line either at the extreme edge of the field or more frequently far enough inside to go between the opposing end and tackle. The principal study of the play is directed towards the proper timing of it, that is, to insure the arrival of first one man, then another, at the previously undefended point just as the runner is passing that point. Theoretically, if one could shift the entire line of forwards toward the end which is being assailed, and keep within that line all the opposing tacklers, he would have a perfect interference for an end-run. But practically the opponents refuse to be thus hemmed in, and it is therefore necessary to form a protection for a space of perhaps five yards, and the protection must move as rapidly as the runner behind it. This protecting mass first strikes out across the field for two reasons—first, to move the play quickly to a point where the heavy centre and guards cannot assist in stopping the runner; and secondly, to allow the runner to get his full speed on. As the protecting mass moves along the line, it reaches a point where the resistance will be weakest, and then presses its weight rapidly in towards the opponents' goal, and the runner performs his circling part, while the one or two interferers he has more closely tied to him either still precede him, or more usually go on towards the opposing end, thus effectually preventing him from coming in to head off the runner. Now, it must be remembered that this protecting mass of men is obliged to meet the assaults of the opponents, and still preserve the impregnability of its line. This they must also do without the use of their hands or arms. There are two distinct ways of performing this duty: one is by moving so rapidly and closely that an opponent cannot dart in between them, and the other by running into the opponent and knocking him out of the way. The former always yields the most successful results, because the mass is thereby kept intact much longer; the latter usually results in the falling out, man for man, of the interferers with the men they stop. It is easy to see, however, that so long as the attacking party cannot replace the men whom the interferers tumble over, the result is almost identical, for the runner finally reaches his end, even though the last interferer go down with the last of the attacking party. Again, even the swift - moving compact interference is apt to lose one or more men on the way to the end, and there is a great deal of labor involved in teaching them to close the ranks in time to prevent the next opponent from taking advantage of it.

Up to very recently the men who went into the interference were drawn from that side of the centre only upon which the play was to be executed; but the possibility of getting the other guard over to assist has already been demonstrated, and the far end as well is now regularly added. Some captains believe in giving each one of their interferers a certain man to take, and it is by far the simplest way to try the play. But it does not follow that it is the best way, and the more recent developments have already consigned this practice to the category of " has-beens " in the football world. It is impossible to give any captain definite advice as to the relative time and speed to set his interferers, because it all hinges upon the individuals involved ; but he must bear in mind one fact, and that is that the interfering mass should increase its speed progressively as it goes towards the end, just as the best runner always puts on steam as he nears the point he is to try to compass. One other question which sometimes arises can only be answered by experiment. It is, How close should the interference be to the runner? It depends not upon the opponents, but upon the individual desire of the runner, and he ought to be the sole judge. Close interference completely upsets and slows some excellent halves, whereas there are men who want to have the interferers literally against them as they run.

As to the men who can get into the interference, it is a cardinal point that every available man should be drawn over if the time admits, but as a rule the opposite guard and a dropped-back end can be carried behind the line. The opposite tackle can get through and take a half-back, as such a player as Newell demonstrated. The order then is two guards, a tackle, and an end, thus giving four men; then, a lively quarter, like Dean, King, and perhaps one or two others, has been able to do effective work in preceding the runner. That gives a line of five (the near end is engaged in boxing the tackle). Then the extra half and back, who are, however, used more frequently in tandem style, are added to the combination, giving a total of seven men. Lewis and Balliet are examples of centre men who can and sometimes do succeed in making their number eight, and any team that can crowd eight men into the interference may consider themselves as coming close up to the limit if the play is to be made fast.

For all this, the development of the game is such that no one can with safety set any limit to the number engaged in an interference play of the future without giving the entire eleven.

THE WEDGE

The wedge, a play which at first was only used at kick-off and kick-out, then a little later upon fair catches, soon became sufficiently attractive, and so eminently successful as to suggest that a modification of it could be made available upon the occasion of ordinary downs. It is quite within the range of possibility to say that one Harvard-Yale match was, in its final result, determined by the advantages possessed by the Yale team of the use of what were then dubbed "small wedges on downs." The touch-down which decided the match was obtained by two or three of these small wedges supplemented by a similar formation, from the side of which a player emerged and crossed the line. Wesleyan in that same year, and a short time after this match between Harvard and Yale, met Pennsylvania, and surprised every one by defeating the Philadelphians by a succession of these small wedges.

Since that time football captains have been devoting more and more attention to this mass work, until in 1893 it bade fair to monopolize too much of the play. Naturally, this means that the wedge or mass play is successful in gaining ground, for no captain uses a play in order to produce an effect upon the spectator. He uses it to gain distance, and the play which can most repeatedly add in three downs five or more yards to his coveted progress, is the play he will bring to the highest pitch of perfection.

If one will bear in mind the features of the ordinary wedge at kick-off, such as described in a previous chapter of this book, he will readily grasp the principle of the smaller wedges on downs. It is to bring a group of men, behind whom is the runner, into contact with such part of the enemy's line as shall be most easily reached and broken through. This group of men must partake in their formation of the nature of a V; that is, there must be concentrated pressure, and in a pre-arranged direction, to insure the success of the play.

The chief difficulty in perfecting wedge work on downs lies in the too great proximity of the opponents. At kick-off, kick-out, and fair catches, it was possible to take sufficient distance not only to perfect the formation, but also to secure momentum before the opposing line was met. There was, therefore, more of the "smashing" character in these wedges where the lines were separated than there can ever be in wedges formed on downs. This the captain or coach should bear constantly in mind in his planning, or his wedges on downs will never be markedly successful. Such wedges depend for their value upon very close formation, and, as it were, a cumulative pressure. The first start of the wedge is more a closing-up than anything else, then comes a very rapidly increasing pressure from behind that lifts the opponents back and crowds ahead for a few yards. A wedge on a down ought never to make over a few yards, although certain outlets for the runner may result in an eventual gain of quite a distance. There are several types of these wedges, the most common being the straight wedge, which forces the centre or guards, and what is called the revolving wedge, which, turning upon itself, may and sometimes does succeed in rolling past the obstructing forces. In all the methods it is customary to snap the ball to the quarter, he being very close up to his centre man and the wedge

being packed in tightly around him before the ball is played; he then hands
it to the runner, who stands within
the wedge, and the mass moves in the
determined direction, either directly
ahead or deflecting to one side or the
other. This latter method is the proper one for revolving wedges, and is far
more successful than the crude attempts
where the players themselves endeavor
by turning around like tops to impart
a revolving motion to the mass itself.
Almost all these wedges depend, unfortunately, upon the use of hands and
arms to hold them together, and there
is a question as to how far this should
be allowed by the umpire. As a matter of fact, so lenient has been the ac-
cepted ruling that it is doubtful if the
opinion of football-players would at
this day support an umpire who ruled
strictly that such interference was ille-

gal, if it prevented the opponents from breaking into the wedge.

The wedge play will continue to be used, but to a more limited extent, and with a probably greater distance of movement before meeting the line. The wedge play is not a mere weight play. It is a play that, when well designed and skilfully executed, has behind it weeks of planning and study. The University of Pennsylvania's wedges were models of skill. The Harvard flying wedge was a piece of clever headwork. The wedges which drove Butterworth through any line that opposed Yale were not mere push-plays. The wedge has a right to stay, and ought to be given a chance. But the wedge has a way of tying up the play to a too limited space; it has a way of exhausting and using up men who face it too many times in succession,

Those outside the lines can seldom see its plan of action; they can only see the mass, and it loses its interest when worked too often. It ought to be *a possible play*, but not *all the play*, and legislation which will induce the captain for the interest of his team to use other plays as well is the legislation that will be productive of the best results in the end.

APPENDIX

TEAM PLAY

IF ever a sport offered inducements to the man of executive ability, to the man who can plan, foresee, and manage, it is certainly the modern American football. Already in the years during which the game has been played in this country the fact has been time and again demonstrated that a team composed of the very pick of individual players has no chance whatever against the systematic methods of even the ordinarily well-drilled team, whose members are by no means equal in attainments or physique to the picked team, but who have played together for months, and whose force can be concentrated on the word at any desired point.

Team play is the road to victory, and the only one in these days of football, when captains and coaches spend far more time and thought over the conduct of the campaign than over individual work. Not only is the general dependence of one man upon another brought out and made a feature of the work, but the general movement of the struggle, the point of pressure, and the lines of resistance—all are become an interesting study for those who mean to win.

Unfortunately the fact that, when the season commences, probably half the men on a team are new militates very strongly against any early attempts at general team-work, but with patience the rudimentary knowledge is drilled into the new recruits, and after a few weeks the coach can begin to teach them uniformity of action as a whole. Of the plays most commonly practised by teams of the present day, there are perhaps a score which one can note as regulation plays, and a brief description of certain of these will aid captains and coaches who have new teams to break in.

THE WEDGE, OR V.

The wedge, or V, is the play formerly used to open a game by probably nine tenths of the teams. Under the later amendments the prevalence of wedge-plays has been greatly lessened, for they can no longer be used where the rules call for a kick; but small wedges on downs are still as available and as effective as ever, so that a thorough understanding of them is necessary. The play takes its name from the peculiar arrangement of the players during the attempt to advance. The formation is that of a V-shaped mass of men, with the runner inside the V. The point is directed towards the enemy's line, and the endeavor is to force an opening through which the runner may emerge, and continue on even after the wedge of protecting men is brought to a standstill. The first point in this play is an actual advance of the entire body by main force of weight and pushing as far as possible, keeping the formation unbroken, so that the runner with the ball may not be stopped. This usually means an appreciable advance. Then there is the additional chance of so separating the opponents as to allow the runner to come out at the peak or through the side suddenly and unexpectedly while the opponents are involved in the mass, and by this unexpected emergence add to the gain made by the wedge an ofttimes unimpeded and considerable run of his own. Some coaches instruct the runner to use his own discretion about selecting his opening; others have a definite understanding as to where he is to emerge, the two men between whom he goes making the opening at the time when they find the wedge stopping. The latter method is far preferable in a well-drilled team whose men are not wofully overmatched by their opponents in respect to size and strength. A team should practise variations of this play in order that the runner may have the

advantage of surprising the opponents by
not coming out at always the same point.
Several modifications of the wedge play
have been practised with more or less success by different teams. One of the most
clever was a one-sided V play in which the
men started off sharply, making a diagonal
line of men running across and against the
opponents, while the man with the ball ran
just behind them, and managed to make the
distance which this line could cut off from
the field.

The wedge and its principles were, of
course, more chiefly applicable when the
opponents were restrained from advancing,
as in kick-off, kick-out, and fair catches, but
the same formation upon a smaller scale is
now largely practised in the case of ordinary downs.

HOW TO MEET A WEDGE.

Many are the ways in which opponents
try to meet and defeat the ends of this

wedge play. The most simple, and the one which has commended itself most generally, is that of lying down before it. It is not deeply scientific, and is sometimes rather trying to those who perform the duty; but it is effective to a degree, and, when there are no other means which seem to check the advance, is not to be scorned. The men in the front of the wedge fall over the prostrate antagonists, and the advance comes to a stop suddenly and surely. But there is an objection in the case of a cleverly manipulated wedge when the runner is helped out at the side, and the men who are down in front cannot rise to be of any assistance in stopping him. Of course there are others upon whom this duty should devolve; but rapid and judicious interference at the proper moment may take these out of the way, and the gain made be far greater than by a direct forcing at the peak of the wedge. Other methods of opposition are : breaking in the peak by main strength; sending a man over the heads of the leaders; and, finally, and more scientific when skilfully performed, holding the peak and turning the pressure off, so that the wedge goes across the field instead of straight ahead.

A SECOND PLAY.

As under the present methods of play, the game is started with an actual kick, and that kick is usually of necessity made against whatever wind there may be, the side receiving the ball is prompted to return it with the wind. Therefore, when the game has been started, and the first kick executed, almost the next manœuvre will be a punt, say by a half-back or back. The team play upon this is to secure the ground gained by the kick. This is only possible by the coincidence of several events —a well-directed kick, strong and rapid following up, aided by slow or careless play by the opponents. But in every case the attempt must be made, and the forwards, par-

ticularly the ends, or, if they be badly impeded, the tackles, must go down the field
hard, upon the chance of getting the ball or
forcing a down, rather than a return kick or
a scratch. Here good judgment plays a
most important part. First, in the kicker.
If he can select the most difficult point for
the half or back of his opponents to reach,
and there place the ball, he gives his own
men a fair chance to make good his kick.
This is also equally applicable to the initial
kick opening the game. If he send the ball
too high, his opponents will surely be able
to reach the spot and secure a fair catch.
If he send it too low, his own men have no
time to get down the field, and the opponents will surely return the kick—probably
on the run, and with interest. A happy
medium between the two is what he must
try for, and it is only long practice which
will enable him to hit upon this happy medium.

FORWARD PLAY UNDER A KICK.

Then, too, the judgment of his forwards
often makes the difference between success
and failure in this play. It must be remembered that the forwards cannot start off
madly down the field as soon as the ball is
snapped. If they could there would be no
difficulty about their being on hand when
the ball came. But each has to block his
man first, in order that the kicker may not
be stopped by a man getting through upon
him while in the very act of kicking the ball.
The usual fault of green forwards is to block
too long, and hence to be late in getting
after the kick. The fault of the older men
is apt to be the opposite one of taking too
great chances for the sake of an early start.
Then there is also a way of telling where the
ball is going to fall by the movement and
faces of the opponents, rather than by stopping to look over one's own head to actually
see the ball itself. Veteran forwards seldom

15

have to see the ball as they go down the field. They can judge exactly from the opponents where to go.

This knack of reading at a glance the probable dropping-point of the kick is acquired by nearly all men who play long in the forward line, and it makes a wonderful difference in the quickness with which they can follow up a kick. But there is one other point often — too often — neglected in the practice, and hence of no manner of use in a game. I refer to an understanding between the forwards and the kicker as to where he intends driving the ball; also as to whether he will send a high kick or a low one; still further, and most important of all, whether he will kick into touch or not. Under the new rules this point becomes of the very greatest importance.

KICKING INTO TOUCH.

One play by no means unpopular of late and likely to become still more attractive was that of deliberately kicking into touch on the third down (or short kicking by the quarter-back) and making a try at recovering the ball. Of course the success of the play depended largely upon whether the opponents were taken by surprise or not; but even when they suspected such a stratagem there was still some chance of success, because they could not place a man over in touch without greatly weakening their defence, and giving a fair opportunity of driving the ball between them in the field of play. When this kicking into long touch upon a third down is attempted, the forwards are always apprised of it. But there is almost as much reason for advising them of the probable destination of the ball in other kicks as well, and before many more seasons the crack teams will have signals that shall convey this needed information fully to the forwards. The reason this development has not come earlier is that the punting of Americans is not up to the standard of the rest of their play. Most strikingly is this true of the accuracy of their punts. When, therefore, a kicker does not know himself where he is going to send the ball, there is no great demand for a signal which would only mean that he might possibly send the ball in a certain direction, but the chances were about even of its going elsewhere. As soon as American teams have half-backs or backs competent to place the ball when they punt it with some fair measure of accuracy, we shall find them signalling the direction of each kick to their forwards. Then will the opposition that may now be advanced against this play with quite a preponderance of success become far more difficult.

DEFEATING A KICK.

At present the team play to defeat the object of a kick consists of sending one or two extra men up into the forward line—one of them the quarter and the other a half if

deemed safe—and then attacking the kicking side at any of the points along which
the ball travels in its course; that is, endeavoring to secure the ball while it is being
snapped to the quarter, while the quarter is
passing it to a half, while the half is catching it, while he is kicking it, and, finally,
just as it starts on its course, before it
passes above the uplifted hands. All this
in the direction of stopping the kick. Next,
as to neutralizing its effect; and here, perhaps, is the less clearly understood portion
of the play. When the ball has passed
safely from the foot of the kicker over the
heads of the attacking forwards, only the
smallest portion of the gain has been effected, and it is possible to entirely neutralize
the play if the action is quick and united.
First, the men who are following up the kick
must be stopped or retarded; and, next, the
man who is about to receive the ball must
be protected. But the style of kick must
determine which of these two elements is of

the greater importance. For instance, if the kick be a high one, and one that does not carry the ball very far down the field, no amount of interference—legitimate interference—can prevent some of the forwards reaching the spot where the ball will fall some time before it comes down. And, again, on a low long kick going directly at the full back, a very slight amount of interference will allow him plenty of time to take the ball and return it, and he may need no protection whatever beyond that which early interference will give to him. And the final point is, of course, the quickness, coolness, and skill of the man who must receive and return the kick either from a fair catch or on the run. As a rule, unless for a chance at goal or a particularly placed kick, the return on the run is the preferred method, because then the forwards are up under the kick, where they, in their turn, may take advantage of the fumbling of an adversary. Then, too, it gives the enemy the larger

share of the running to do. A fair catch
recalls the forwards to "on side," and gives
the opponents a chance to rearrange their
scattered men, as well as a clear field in
which to catch and return.

BUCKING THE LINE.

The simplest form of team play (and even
in these days of highly developed interference it is worth while to study the
method of a simple play) in "a run" is
that wherein a half-back attempts to make
his way through the line at some given point.
Let us take, for the sake of an example, a
run between guard and tackle. The principal feature of this play, and yet the one
most regularly neglected, is to get the runner up into the line in good form and with
the ball well held. Three out of every five
failures of this play come from a cause op-
erating before the runner strikes the line.
The ball may be badly passed to him, he
may be too slow in starting, he may fumble

the ball when it comes, or he may hesitate
or even drop the ball just before he reaches
the line. Any one of these mistakes may
serve to bring a man upon his back before he
takes his plunge. But there are faults which
are not to be attributed to the runner, yet just
as fatal to his success, although they are the
work, or rather lack of work, of others. Any
man along the line may let his opponent
through, and that opponent be able to reach
the runner from behind before he can make
his opening. The likeliest places for this to
happen are on the opposite side at tackle,
and sometimes, in the case of an extra man,
like a quarter, near the centre. The first
lesson for the coach, then, to teach his pu-
pils regarding this play is the absolute necessity of blocking sharply until the runner can start. It is not necessary to hold a
man until the runner has gone through ; it is
only necessary to block long enough to be
sure that the man let through will be too
late to reach the runner. As to the men who

are engaged in making the opening, they must be unanimous in their action. If the guard pushes his man out of the way a minute before the tackle disposes of his man, the runner will never be able to get through safely. The two men must act at the same instant, and merely force their men apart, rather than attempt, as some forwards do, to carry the opponent ten yards or so out of the way. The most successful opening is not the large one, but the small, sharply defined one that just lets the runner through, and lets nobody through behind him. From this, one must see that the calculation of the proper time to make the opening is rather a delicate matter. That it certainly is; for, made too early, it is sure to become choked before the runner reaches it; and made too late, it delays him so that he is caught from behind. It ought to come just as his footsteps bring him up to it. In fact, it has not been badly described as appearing to be made by a "cow-catcher" preceding him by a few feet.

THE TANDEM PLAY.

This idea has been carried into execution by making an accompanying half act as a "cow-catcher," preceding the runner through the opening to clear the way, and in many cases to be tackled by mistake for the holder of the ball, who is thus enabled to make on a few steps farther. This play, with its general application to runs made through the rush line, has been known as the "tandem play," and is often diversified by having a third man still take part in it by joining his comrade in preceding the runner, or else by following after the runner, and giving him a much-needed push when he seems likely to come to a standstill. The chief caution to give the assistants in this tandem play is that if they precede the runner, they must not under any circumstances fall down or allow themselves to be thrown to the ground. If a leader finds himself losing his balance, and realizes that he cannot regain his feet, but must tumble, his last attempt

must be to throw himself—and, if possible,
an opponent—clear of the path he knows
his runner is likely to need.

SPOILING A RUN.

And this indicates what the opposition is
that should be advanced to meet this play.
As in the case of a kick, every attempt
should be made to spoil the quarter's pass,
to prevent the half from receiving the ball
safely, and, finally, to overtake him before he
reaches, or just as he has entered, his opening.   In order to make this last attempt
more successful, there should be a general
understanding among those near the play
that they must "choke up the opening" at
all hazards, by getting into it themselves
or by throwing an opponent there.   It is
well to remember that if, by mistake, a man
tackles the one who hasn't the ball, he has
still done good service if, by so doing, he
has blocked the way of the runner; whereas
if he tackle the man in this way, and throw

him to one side instead of into the opening, he has aided the runner.

After the runner has gone through the line, and is making his way down the field, every rusher should feel it his duty to follow him, no matter how hopeless the chase may at the moment appear to be. There is always a chance of overtaking the runner, even if he have no one to pass ; and in this case he will probably have to go by two men at least, one half and the back. Here is also a point which the coach should thoroughly instil into the minds of his halves and back, and that is the advisability of going forward to meet the runner rather than waiting for him to come. There are two reasons for this act, both of them sound ones. In the first place, if the tackle prove successful, the gain made by the run will be shortened by just the amount that the tackler advanced ; and, secondly, if it prove unsuccessful, it nevertheless increases the opportunities for still overtaking the runner, both by upsetting his calculations in regard to his direction, and by giving him less time to think how he shall make his turn.

END RUN.

The next distinctive team play of im-portance is an end run. Usually one of the backs is the man selected for the great-er part of this work, and in the execution of it clever interference reaches its height. Not that the interference itself is more difficult in this play than in any other, but that the massing of men at the point of attack is more long-continued, and hence must be planned not as a single instant of combined pressure, but as several minutes of running interference. When well performed, it looks like the swinging of a long line of men against the flank of the opponents, as one might swing a line of boys in "snap the whip," and one, the runner, goes spinning off around the end just as the lines seem to meet. All this is in appearance only, for to accomplish the play successfully several men must be checked or interfered with as the runner makes his way out to the end; and just as he reaches that point, and puts on his burst of speed, there must be a clever shutting-off of the outermost man. Such work cannot be learned in a day. It requires the steady practice together of the same men for weeks before the precision of movement can be attained. All teams do not carry out the end play in exactly the same manner, and it is by no means certain that any particular method may be selected and called the best of them all. But whatever the method is, it must be practised faithfully, its weaknesses patched up, and its movement regulated, if it is to prove a success when the important time of trial comes; that is, in actual contest with a strange and strong team.

EXECUTION OF AN END RUN.

The description of a single method will suffice to show the chief points of the play, and will indicate the lines upon which it should be built. Let us suppose that the coach chooses to send the left half-back around the right end. Even the most ignorant of football novices will appreciate the fact that such a play is mere madness if the ball is well over on the right side of the field, for then the runner would only be going straight into the very thickest of the crowd, and with clear space ahead only after he should have gone outside the touch line. The first thing to be done, then, is to select an opportunity or make one when the ball shall be well over upon the left side of the field. Then give the signal for this play, and let the left half-back, as soon as the ball is snapped, start towards the right, receiving the ball, and then running directly across the field ten yards or less behind the line of forwards. At the same moment the right half-back and back make off in a similar direction, but, from the advantage of their position, preceding the runner by a few yards.

The quarter, too, immediately after passing the ball, runs to the right, very much nearer the forward line, however, than any of the other three, and in such a way as to jostle off any man who may have succeeded in getting through the line of rushers. The left guard goes with the quarter, and the left end has dropped back and starts almost with the left half. The guard, tackle, and end on the right are meantime blocking their men as well as they can; and it is easy to understand that, as soon as these men see the direction of the runner, they will endeavor to get over to the right end as rapidly as their encumbered position will allow. The result is that the entire side of the line moves in that direction; but as each opponent is impeded to a greater or less degree by the man who is blocking him, the runner and his two preceding comrades are making much better time towards the desired gap that intervenes between the end of the rush line and the edge of the field. When the runner finds himself approaching a point a few yards inside the opposing end, he puts on his highest speed, and tries to circle the end of the line. At the same moment his two comrades have reached that end, and, by interfering, crowd into the field any opponent who has succeeded in reaching a dangerous proximity to the side line. As the runner goes past the extreme end, the combined force of his half and back with the end and tackle, and perhaps a quarter as well, compresses the line of straggling opponents into a kind of cramped semicircle, outside of which the runner has a fairly good chance of a long run. The principal element is not the number of men who are engaged, but the proper timing of their interference to so tangle up the opposing line, as the runner makes for the end, that, when he makes his spurt, he shall have a fair chance, by the use of his highest speed, to pass the narrow gap without being tackled or forced into touch.

MEETING AN END RUN.

The opposition to this end run is based upon two things—one, the activity of the general line in breaking through and reaching the runner; the other, the cleverness of the end in avoiding the interferers and guarding the edge of the field. It would seem perfectly simple for a coach to instruct an end to stand at his post, close to the touch line, and thus block up the gap; but if that be performed too literally, the runner turns earlier and comes inside the end, making his run just as effective as though he passed outside. Green men on the end err, as a rule, far oftener on the side of coming in too far or too soon than they do in sticking too closely to the touch line; so that in coaching green men it is better to keep them for some time under the strictest orders to make the runner go on the inside. Later, when they have mastered the idea that there is nothing to help them on the outside except a slender touch line, they can be gradually permitted to exercise a little judgment on their own account in the matter of leaving the side line in case of emergency. The truth of the matter is that so much depends upon thorough co-operation between an end and his own tackle, that the two should be law each to the other. No other method of play, such as laying down a hard and fast rule as to when an end may try for a man, can ever meet with the success that can be brought about by a thorough understanding and playing in pairs of these two positions.

ADAPTATION OF THE FOUR PLAYS.

These plays—the wedge, the kick, the run through the line, and the run around the end —make a framework upon which a coach may build up an almost endless variety of movements; and if he follow the points laid down for the successful execution of these, he will find that they act as guides to almost any manœuvre he may wish to attempt.

For example, the principle of the wedge may be adapted to almost any forcing *en masse*, no matter at what point it may be directed. Similarly, the blocking for a punt is not very unlike that to be adopted when a drop-kick is attempted. All running by half-backs through the line takes on the character of either the run between guard and tackle or that around the end, while the assistance rendered by interferers is usually either that shown in the tandem play or that illustrated in the end run.

TEAM TACTICS.

But there is still another branch to be discussed, which might be classed under the head of team tactics rather than that of team play. That branch is the study of transferring the play from point to point, and the adaptation of the various methods to the end immediately desired. One can readily see that a team might be proficient in all the plays described, and be composed of good material, and yet, by a failure to use the right play at the proper time, make a most pitiable showing. To take an extreme case, a team might be directly under the opponent's goal and within a few yards of the goal line, with the ball at first down, and, instead of forcing the ball over or trying a drop, might let a half or back punt the ball over the line, and thus give the opponents a touch back and the privilege of bringing the ball out to the twenty-five-yard line. Or, again, a team might have a strong wind at their backs, and the ball be down in their own goal at the third down. Instead of driving a long punt down the field, they might send a runner ploughing up into the line, and, making no gain, be obliged to surrender the ball to their opponents. Such generalship, while it seems, when studied in cold blood, absolutely idiotic, is in minor ways regularly exhibited a dozen times in a game by captains who ought to know better.

USING THE WIND.

The study of the best methods of taking advantage of the wind is one of the most important, particularly now that kicking has been increased in importance, and will reward the captain and coach fully as much as the same amount of thought expended upon any other feature of the game. The majority are contented with the mere knowledge that the side which has the wind should do the most kicking, but in reality such a statement of the case is wholly inadequate. When the wind is blowing straight down the field, its value as a factor in the kicking game is something which spectators scarcely realize, and even the players themselves hardly reckon at its full account until they are compelled to face it. But, for all this, one must not conclude that the thing to do is to punt the ball as far down the field as possible every time the opportunity offers. Especially is such a policy a poor one when

the ball is near enough to the opponents'
goal to make the kick send it past the goal
line. A drop kick under such circumstances
is sometimes, though not always, indicated.
If it is a first-down inside the twenty-five-
yard line, it is generally advisable; because
then the opponents can have only to the
ten-yard line for their kick-out, and must,
moreover, kick out against the wind. The
true way to make use of the wind under
these conditions depends oftentimes upon
the stage of the game at the moment. If the
runners on the team are fresh and strong,
and from their earlier attempts have shown
that they can repeatedly succeed in making
their five yards, it is frequently advisable
when within the fifteen yard line to play
for a touch-down. But, on the other hand,
if there be only a few minutes of playing
time left, and five points will turn a defeat
into victory, the drop kick may be strongly
called for.

KICKING INTO TOUCH NEAR GOAL LINE.

But chiefest of all, in a game where the sides are fairly well matched and the game in its early stages, is the kick into touch near the corner. American players seem as yet to have gained no great knowledge of the immense value of this kicking into touch. An English back will seldom kick anywhere else than into touch, while our players do not even realize the value of such a kick in the most marked cases. When the ball is still far from the goal, and yet so within the enemy's territory as with the wind to make it likely that a strong kick will send it to the goal line, the play should always be to kick into touch as well down towards the corner as possible. Such a play puts the opponents upon the defensive, and that, too, in a most unpleasant manner, for it brings them up against their own goal with a course and two alternatives from which to choose. They must, by wonderful running, gain their five yards more than once, or be forced to kick directly before their own goal, or finally make a safety touchdown. If they make a safety, it gives their enemies two points ; if they kick the ball, it gives their enemies a more than fair chance to catch the ball, heel it, and place kick a goal. If they try a run, it may turn into a safety. And it is by no means an encouraging situation for a runner called upon to carry the ball out of such a predicament. The side which is forced is likely to be discouraged, while the attacking side is doubly confident and strong from their close proximity to the opponents' goal.

WHEN AND WHERE TO KICK.

But this is only a very simple case, and the reasons for the play are evident. There are many other occasions where there is more opportunity for discussion ; for instance, the question whether, when with the wind, it is always advisable to kick on the first down.

One of the best rules to follow in this case is that a captain can safely send his men occasionally for a run on first downs, or even second downs, so long as he only gives them enough work to keep them active, and not to tire them in the least. He should always remember that one of the chief advantages to be gained from the wind is that of keeping his own runners fresh by kicking, while his opponents are obliged to exhaust their men by making their recovery of lost ground almost entirely by running. One rule when playing with the wind the captain is never justified in breaking, so long as he is not close to the opponents' goal, and that is to "get in his kick." In other words, no matter if he has gained in his two attempts all but six inches of the five yards, he must take no chances of another run when the wind is with him, but kick.

A point sometimes forgotten is that in important matches the crowd are often so arranged upon the stands as to shut off much of the force of the wind in the lower strata of the air, and for this reason as well a kick with the wind should be a high kick. For the same reason, the side which is facing the wind should always, when forced to kick, send the ball rather low, and as hard as possible.

THE EFFECT OF THE CHANGES IN RULES

In no sport so much as football does a slight alteration in a rule effect such remarkable changes in the style of play. When, therefore, a number of essentially radical alterations are introduced and a general revision made, as has been done lately, there can be little doubt of our seeing some remarkable effects. Many of them will be agreeable to the spectator and probably to a considerable proportion of the players, although the older players are always conservative about any alterations in a rule. Perhaps, therefore, it is well at the outset of this chapter to state the reasons which led to this general revision.

The tendency developed in the last three

or four years towards more closeness of play led to an over-reliance by the captains upon wedge and mass plays of all descriptions. This was only natural, because it was by means of these plays that possession of the ball could be most advantageously continued. Except at opening plays, these methods were not productive of long gains or brilliant runs, but partook of a general hammering nature, yielding, however, enough to make the five yards in three downs. No one could afford to ignore the fact that in close, hard-fought games, and particularly in rainy weather, these were the safest tactics to adopt. But all this meant a general disregard of the kicking game and the sacrifice of long passes and brilliant methods to something which should be safer in the captain's eye. The interest of the spectator, and especially the interest of the spectator who was fairly versed in the game, began to wane under these conditions, and there was a great deal of dissatisfaction felt even with the play of 1892. When all these faults be-came still more exaggerated in 1893, there was a loud call for action of some kind; and by the time the season was ended players and the public were ready for, at any rate, the first steps towards the curtail-ment of the close play and a reintroduction of the more open kicking methods. The University Athletic Club, at the invitation of some of the leading colleges, appointed a committee of experts, who held meetings during the winter and spring, and in May proposed a set of rules which were accept-ed by the University Athletic Club, and adopted to govern the Harvard-Yale con-test, and later by the Intercollegiate Asso-ciation.

So far for an explanation of the causes which led to the first general revision. A second took place in 1896. The effect upon the play no one can be sure of. The wedge and mass plays will undoubtedly

still be continued, though not to so great
an extent; and the kicking will surely not
be, as a great many have supposed, the
entire feature of the contest in the future.
It will take more severe legislation to bring
such a change as that about. The game
will, however, open with a kick, and very
likely, when there is much wind, with two
kicks—that is, the winner of the toss, having his choice of goal or kick-off, will
probably take goal, and the opponents will,
therefore, have the kick-off. The new rules
provide that this kick-off must be an actual
kick into the opponent's territory of, at
least, ten yards, so that it is probable that
we shall see the old-fashioned start once
more. But the side receiving the ball,
having the wind with them, will be inclined
to take an early opportunity of returning
the kick, so that, as stated above, we shall
probably see two kicks early in the game.
The running play may even be deferred
until the ball has been thus kicked and

returned, and the opening play, by the
holder's flying wedge or an attempt made
to hold the ball through a succession of
downs until a touch-down is secured, has
been done away with. The final difference,
however, will not be very great, because
after the return kick the side playing
against the wind will then naturally endeavor to play a running game and hold
the ball as long as possible. To sum up
the first few minutes of the game, therefore,
it is not unlikely that we shall see the side
which started off in possession of the ball
beginning their running game, instead of at
the middle of the field, some ten or fifteen
yards back of that centre, dependent, of
course, upon the force of the wind, and beginning with a down instead of with the flying wedge.

Having gone thus far into the game, the
effect of the more stringent rule against
fouls will be of interest. Instead of five
yards, the penalty has been increased to

ten yards for fouls and violation of the
rules, unless the offending side has the
ball, in which case the penalty is the same
as of old—that is, an immediate surrender
of the ball to the opponents. This at
once brings a new element into the game,
because the penalty for a foul to the side
holding the ball is no greater than it was a
year ago, but the penalty inflicted upon the
side acting on the defence is doubled. Just
what the final outcome of this will be is hard
to say ; but the first year shows that it ben-
efits the attack, and so, perhaps, makes it
easier to retain possession of the ball and
make distance. It is certain that it has
tended to make the captain drill his men to
a very strict observation of the rules when
on the defence. So far, then, we find that
the captain and coach now have to educate
their men for good general kicking ; and by
"good" is meant not only long place kicking, but a development of accuracy as well,
and an even more rapid following up of the

17

play than ever before. Then the captain must hold his men under the greatest restraint, to prevent their getting off side during the scrimmage when the opponents have the ball.

The next point we come to is that of the fair catch. Here a provision has been made that, while giving the catcher protection if he so desires it, still permits him to take the chance in a great many kicks of a run with the ball. Of course, when it is a high kick, or he is surrounded by his opponents, he will take the catch and heel the ball; but he is not likely to decide until the last moment, and then he will heel only when there is no chance for a run. To tell the truth, the half-backs and backs are really not so afraid of being thrown as they are of muffing the ball, for all the pity which has been bestowed upon them in the past.

Apropos of these offences, the third official or linesman proves of considerable assistance to the umpire and referee on fouls

as well as on timing the game. He will
probably confine his work mostly to the
side lines, in keeping track of the downs
and distance covered. This, as well as all
his other conduct, is, however, under the
advice of the umpire or the referee, and he
is, therefore, by no manner of means as important an official as either of these.

Fields are now kept clear by a rule which
provides that only one man, and he presum-
ably competent to take care of an injured
player, shall go upon the field in case of an
accident.

When the ball goes into touch we now
see no more scrimmages on the side of the
field as we have at times, for the player cannot bound it in and run with it, but he must
either walk out and put it down in accord-
ance with the most common fashion, or
touch it in and kick it. This latter play is
seldom seen, and "fairs" have probably
resolved themselves into what they have
been practically for the last few years—

namely, a down fifteen yards from the side line.

The effect of limiting the time of the game to an hour and ten minutes has been to make the playing faster and even more dashing than formerly, for it accents the duty of the captains to get all the play possible out of their men in the two shortened halves. Moreover, no time being allowed to recover breath tends to keep the play going with such continuity that spectators are hardly bored by the slowness of the progress.

Perhaps the most important change in methods appears when the ball goes inside the twenty-five-yard line of either goal. In the case where it is in the possession of the defenders of the goal, they strive very hard to retain possession of it, or to surrender it to the other side at some point outside of the twenty-five-yard line. Where, on the other hand, it is in possession of the attacking side, if their running game is not working very well, they are tempted to

resort at once to a drop kick, because by
the new rule if that kick fails the opponents
can bring the ball out only to the ten-yard
line instead of the twenty-five-yard line.
The fact is at once plain that this really
means a kick out from behind one's own
goal, and in addition to this it must be a
kick, for the defenders of the side cannot run
the ball out. This, like the rule increasing
the distance for fouls, is hard on the de-
fending side, and has already resulted in
more scoring than formerly.

The rule limiting mass plays is not sufficiently strong to curtail them very materially, but it will take off some of the extra
weight which has been used in these plays
in the past, and in that way will be of service. While no men can get in motion
before the ball is snapped, the runner is
joined by others who stand still until the
ball is actually put in play, so that while
we shall not see six or seven men at ten or
fifteen yards back starting in a mass and

getting under full headway before the ball is snapped, we shall undoubtedly see three men bunched and being joined by others upon their approaching the line. The ordinary flying wedge at the opening play and on fair catches is, however, relegated to the background by the rule that the ball must be actually kicked, so that we shall see these mass plays used only on downs.

A general survey of the situation leads one to believe that the cardinal points of the play will remain very much the same; that, in fact, the men who have thoroughly learned their positions in the past few years will be the best men for the new methods, because the new methods are only the cutting out of the exaggerated faults that have come in in the last two years. Coaches will find it necessary to have on their teams not only runners but kickers, and the education of the rush line cannot be left merely to mass plays and pushing, but must consist of an intimate knowledge of the possibilities of a kicking game and the way to hold the ground gained by kicks as well as how to defend their own side. How to use the kick-off will continue to be a very interesting problem, as will also whether to make a fair catch or not. There certainly will be times when it will be more advantageous for a man not to make a fair catch than to make it. Then, too, at what particular point to try a drop kick when inside the twenty-five-yard line is likely to make plenty of study.

For the early practice and preliminary work in the game under these changed conditions a few suggestions may be serviceable.

While it will be quite practicable for a team desiring to do so to continue the running game to the absolute exclusion of any open playing, and while such a team, if well drilled and expert in their team work, will be almost as dangerous to face as ever, there has been enough of a premium placed upon kicking to make it unsafe for a team in the first class to ignore that feature. Almost the first thing to do, then, is to provide that among the candidates for the team there may be enough kicking-halves and full-backs to last through the season for both sides—" the 'varsity " and " the scrub." Something of a kicking game should be practised daily, to the exclusion for a time of the running play—say for fifteen or twenty minutes. A team to play a really effective kicking game must, in addition to having the punters able to place their kicks with accuracy, be equipped with a set of signals by means of which the forwards may know the direction and approximately the distance of the kick. Short kicks and putting the men on side will become again worthy of consideration. Kicking into touch will assume more of the importance it holds in the English Rugby Union. Kicking by the quarter—such as was done years ago by Mason of Harvard, and more lately practised by the University of Pennsylvania team and others—will continue to gain in importance. All these plays can be used in combination with the running game, but to develop them up to the level of the play will mean hard work. Still another feature of the game entailed by this kicking method will be the greater necessity for pace among the forwards. How the heavy men of our present forward lines will stand the more rapid progress up and down the field that a very lively interchange of kicks, should they take place, might mean, is a grave question. But it will never do to lighten up the line very much so long as the opponents have the right to send any crushing force of several interferers in front of the runner, for heavy men alone can stand the frequent meeting of such onslaughts.

It will be well for the captains and coachers to once again consider a more general passing game—more of the short-passing of the English player when tackled, as well as such doubles and long passes as Princeton showed the possibility of accomplishing even under the rules of 1893. A short pass for a return kick when the back, catching the ball, is not yet tackled, but too hard pressed to get in his kick, is worth a reintroduction.

For all this style of play, and one hopes its development will be considerable, life and activity are essential, and it is but fair to warn the over-zealous captains against working their men too hard. It will be even a more serious error "to take the edge off" a team before its final effort under the new rules than under the old. Work enough to develop the skill, but not enough to take the heart out of the men, will be the only way to make a first-class team. The exaggerated features of summer training will, it is to be devoutly hoped, yield to a better sense in a few years, and instead of having men tired of the play before mid-season, we shall find them as eager as ever up to the very end.

THE alterations in rules effected by the Rules Committee called together by the University Athletic Club during the spring and summer of 1896 will materially modify some of the situations in the play, and it is proper to carefully consider just what the result of these changes will be.

The rule first to attract our attention is that regarding fair catch. Under this rule in its altered form the man about to catch the ball will come up under it with the privilege of exercising his own judgment as to what line of play he shall adopt as soon as the ball settles in his hands. He may make a fair catch and therefrom take a free kick, or he may run with the ball. Besides this he is protected as effectually as he was in the days when obliged to raise his hand to indicate that he was going to make the catch. Should any one interfere with him, or throw him after he has made the catch, he will receive in addition to his free kick a distance of fifteen yards. In determining what his play shall be he must consider that a fair catch—or, rather, a free kick from a fair catch—is worth more by ten yards than it was under the old rule of two years ago, because the rule of 1896 provides that the opponents must retire ten yards back from the catcher's mark. Formerly it was the catcher who retired ten yards from his mark, or in that neighborhood. This rule ought to work well, in that it puts a heavy penalty on interfering with the man who has made the fair catch, and also adds to the value of the catch by this additional distance. With all this it does not take away from the back the advantage to be gained by quick judgment and a good perception of the chance for a run.

To pass on to the next alteration in the

rules.   It is one which was practically
adopted last year—viz.: that when there is
a fumble in the scrimmage any player may
drop upon the ball; that is, on a fumble
in the scrimmage no man is " off-side."

The next alteration comes in the line of
the umpire and referee.   All sorts of plans
have been tried to insure satisfactory rulings
in our matches, and it seems to be the con-
sensus of opinion, as indicated by the votes
of the representatives forming the Rules
Committee, that by distributing the duties
of the umpire and referee a little more fairly better results will be obtained.   The umpire has, it is true, had of late years a great
deal to do, and only the best men, and perhaps the lucky men, have come off with
anything more than a remnant of their rep-
utations.   The referees have always es-
caped because their duties were not nearly
so arduous.   In order to even this up, and
accomplish more with the same number of
men, it has been determined that the referee

shall act as judge of whether the ball is
fairly put in play, assuming at the same
time the responsibility for seeing that the
snapper-back is not interfered with, nor the
ball touched while he is endeavoring to
put it in play or holding it on the ground
for that purpose. The referee is also
obliged to judge whether the ball is passed
forward, and, finally, whether the quarter-
back runs with it. This leaves the umpire
free to watch the line, and to give his attention to unfair tactics, off-side, and holding.

The next rule altered is that regarding
the runner being fairly held. For a long
time the words "fairly held" have done
duty, and pretty satisfactory duty too ; but
in the last season there have been some
questions raised as to what fairly held
meant, and the rule has, therefore, been expanded by the use of the words " the movement of the ball stopped." This means
evidently that the runner must be tackled
and brought to a standstill, and at the same

time the ball so held that he cannot immediately pass it. Practically, however, this
has always been the rule.

The next alteration in the rules is in that
regarding scrimmage, and this now enacts
that the opponents must not only refrain
from touching the ball when it is being put
in play in the scrimmage, but also that they
must not push or jostle the snap-back.
This had become a very necessary rule, for
there was a great deal of interference with
the centre man, and the tendency seemed
to be on the increase; nor are the opponents allowed to drag men off-side, or do
anything to delay putting the ball in play.

Another rule which has been necessarily
expanded in an explanatory way is that regarding a kick, and what "fair and equal
chance of possession" means. This has
been brought about by the tendency towards
quarter-back kicking and general short
kicking. A quarter-back has sometimes
kicked the ball not alone on a line with

himself, but even slightly backward, in order
to save his side from surrendering possession of it to the opponents on the last down.
Such a kick has usually been properly ruled
upon by the referee or umpire as not giving
the opponents fair and equal chance, but
misunderstandings have not been unheard
of, and the new rule is a good one and
makes it quite clear. The kick must be
past the line of scrimmage; that is, it
must go beyond an imaginary line passing
through the spot where the ball was down,
and drawn at right angles to the side-line,
in order to be regarded as giving the opponents fair and equal chance of possession.

Still another rule has been altered which
deals with a similar case. It is that regarding a kick by the snap-back. It has
always been the privilege of the snap-back,
if he so desired, to kick the ball forward
instead of snapping it back. This was
another method of putting it in play. But
some discussion has arisen as to how far he

must kick it, and what the privileges of himself and his side are in the matter of picking up the ball after such a kick.   The
doubt has been set at rest by enacting a
rule that if the snap-back kick the ball it
must go at least ten yards into the opponents' territory unless stopped by an opponent.   This will probably mean the practical elimination of snap-back kicks, although
there is a chance, when a careless opponent
does not come up at the moment the ball is
down, for a lively snap-back to kick the ball
ahead, as of old.

The rule which, next to that of fair catch,
has always been of the greatest importance,
and has aroused the most discussion, is
that of the scrimmage and the formations
admitted.   A number of years ago the introduction of momentum plays brought a
new element into the game, and one which
for a time seemed likely to add to the interest and the skill.   Unfortunately the tendency grew too rapidly, and with this growth

came unexpected and unwelcome complications in the way of injuries and close "battering-ram" plays. Such an impression did this make that the public arose and insisted upon the elimination of the momentum play. The public here spoken of was not the general public alone, but a great many of the old football-players, and some even of the modern school. What the result of an argument between the two parties might have been if the debate had been decided on its merits one cannot say; but at any rate the first attempt of the Rules Committee some two years ago was directed towards the elimination of both mass and momentum plays. Last year, owing to a split in the ranks, there were two different sets of rules, and under one set some momentum plays were admissible. This year the momentum play has been absolutely extirpated by the passage of a rule forbidding any one to take more than one step in advance before the ball is put in play. One

man of the side may, however, be running
towards his own goal if he so elect when
the ball is put in play. This players will
recognize at once as admitting of quick
change of apparent intention from a supposed running formation into that for a
kick. With this the only exception and
with such a ruling against starting it is
impossible for momentum plays to begin
again.

Next as to mass plays. We find these
not legislated against with anything like the
severity directed against the momentum
play. A mass play is still possible, although
by the new rule it will be more difficult to
make very heavy mass plays with men
bunched closely in the centre. It will not
be impossible to get men into formation after
the ball is put in play so that small mass
plays can be attempted all along the line.
But five men cannot bunch directly behind
the quarter and all push together through
or over the centre. The rule provides that

five men shall be on the line of the scrimmage, and that, if five men besides the quarter go back, two of these shall be either five
yards or more back of the line of scrimmage,
or else shall occupy positions outside what
is known as the tackle position. It will be
seen by the ruling that any man in the line
may be dropped back so long as five men
continue in the line, and the five who drop
back conform to the requirements of the
rule as to the positions they assume.

To sum up briefly the effect of these alterations upon the play itself, one may say,
with a fair measure of prophetic vision :

First. That the putting the ball in play
during the season of 1896 will be cleaner
and more free from the disagreeable features
of scrapping in the line than ever before.

Second. That no momentum plays will
be seen.

Third. That mass plays will be made,
more or less, and that they will be put

against the tackle position with probably the greatest vigor as well as the most likely chance of success.

Finally, that all kicking, and especially quarter-back kicking, will be indulged in with greater freedom, and that general "on side" and short kicks will be used when the side finds it difficult to gain ground with their running game.

To the captains it can be said that no study will prove more profitable in the way of developing a team than that of quick small mass formations, made effective by double passes or sudden changes of direction. While, for a kicking game, accuracy, both in distance and direction, coupled with the ability to kick while on the run, ought to be a feature of the full-back's play more than ever before.

RECORDS SINCE THE INTRODUCTION OF RUGBY GAME.

HARVARD–YALE.

1876. Yale, 1 goal ; Harvard, 2 touch-downs.

1877. No game.

1878. Yale, 1 goal ; Harvard, 0.

1879. Yale, 2 safeties ; Harvard, 4 safeties.

1880. Yale, 1 goal, 1 touch-down ; Harvard, 0.

1881. Yale, 0 ; Harvard, 4 safeties.

1882. Yale, 1 goal, 3 touch-downs ; Harvard, 2 safeties.

1883. Yale, 4 goals ; Harvard, 1 touch-down, 1 safety.

1884. Yale, 6 goals, 4 touch-downs ; Harvard, 0.

1885. No game.

1886. Yale, 5 goals ; Harvard, 1 touch-down.

1887. Yale, 3 goals, 1 safety ; Harvard, 1 goal.

1888. No game.

1889. Yale, 1 goal ; Harvard, 0.

1890. Harvard, 2 goals ; Yale, 1 goal.

1891. Yale, 1 goal, 1 touch-down ; Harvard, 0.

1892. Yale, 1 goal ; Harvard, 0.

1893. Yale, 1 goal ; Harvard, 0.

1894. Yale, 12 ; Harvard, 4.

1895. No game.

HARVARD–PRINCETON.

1876. No game.

1877. Harvard, 1 goal, 1 touch-down ; Princeton, 1 touch-down.

1878. Princeton, 1 touch-down ; Harvard, 0.

1879. Princeton, 1 goal, 1 safety ; Harvard, 5 safeties.

1880. Princeton, 2 goals, 2 touch-downs, 6 safeties ; Harvard, 1 goal, 1 touch-down, 4 safeties.

1881. Princeton, 1 safety ; Harvard, 1 safety.

1882. Harvard, 1 goal, 1 touch-down; Princeton, 1 goal.

1883. Princeton, 26 points ; Harvard, 7 points.

1884. Princeton, 34 points ; Harvard, 6 points.

1885. No game.

1886. Princeton, 12 points ; Harvard, 0.

1887. Harvard, 12 points ; Princeton, 0.

1888. Princeton, 18 points ; Harvard, 6 points.

1889. Princeton, 41 points ; Harvard, 15 points.

1890. No game.

1891. No game.

1892. No game.

1893. No game.

1894. No game.

1895. Princeton, 12 ; Harvard, 4.

PRINCETON–YALE.

1876. Yale, 2 goals ; Princeton, 0.

1877. Yale, 2 touch-downs ; Princeton, 0.

1878. Princeton, 1 goal ; Yale, 0.

1879. Yale, 2 safeties ; Princeton, 5 safeties.

1880. Yale, 5 safeties ; Princeton, 11 safeties.

1881. Yale, 0 ; Princeton, 0.

1882. Yale, 2 goals, 1 safety ; Princeton, 1 goal, 1 safety.

1883. Yale, 1 goal ; Princeton, 0.

1884. Yale, 1 goal ; Princeton, 1 touch-down.*

1885. Princeton, 1 goal from touch-down ; Yale, 1 goal from field.

1886. Yale, 1 touch-down ; Princeton, 0.*

1887. Yale, 2 goals ; Princeton, 0.

1888. Yale, 2 goals ; Princeton, 0.

1889. Princeton, 1 goal, 1 touch-down ; Yale, 0.

1890. Yale, 32 points ; Princeton, 0.

1891. Yale, 19 points, 2 goals, 2 touch-downs ; Princeton, 0.

1892. Yale, 12 points, 2 goals ; Princeton, 0.

* Game unfinished.

1893. Princeton, 6 points, 1 goal ; Yale, 0.

1894. Yale, 24 ; Princeton, 0.

1895. Yale, 20 ; Princeton, 10.

UNIVERSITY OF PENNSYLVANIA–WESLEYAN.

1884. Univ. of Pa., 14 points ; Wesleyan, 12 points.

1885. Univ. of Pa., 18 points ; Wesleyan, 25 points.

1886. Univ. of Pa., 14 points ; Wesleyan, 0.

1887. Univ. of Pa., 4 points ; Wesleyan, 10.

1888. Univ. of Pa., 18 points ; Wesleyan, 6 points.

1889. Univ. of Pa., 2 points ; Wesleyan, 10 points.

1890. Univ. of Pa., 16 points ; Wesleyan, 10 points.

1891. Univ. of Pa., 18 points ; Wesleyan, 10 points.

1892. Univ. of Pa., 34 points ; Wesleyan, 0.

UNIVERSITY OF PENNSYLVANIA–HARVARD.

1883. Univ. of Pa., 0 ; Harvard, 4.

1884. Univ. of Pa., 4 ; Harvard, 0.

1885. Did not play.

1886. Univ. of Pa., 0 ; Harvard, 28.

1889. Univ. of Pa., 0 ; Harvard, 35.

1893. Univ. of Pa., 4 ; Harvard, 26.

1894. Univ. of Pa., 18 ; Harvard, 4.

1895. Univ. of Pa., 17 ; Harvard, 14.

UNIVERSITY OF PENNSYLVANIA–YALE.

1879. Univ. of Pa., 0 ; Yale, 3 goals, 5 touch-downs.

1880. Univ. of Pa., 0 ; Yale, 8 goals, 1 touch-down.

1885. Univ. of Pa., 1 goal, 2 safeties ; Yale, 4 goals, 7 touch-downs.

1886. Univ. of Pa., o ; Yale, 8 goals, 7 touch-downs.

1887. Univ. of Pa., 1 safety ; Yale, 6 goals, 3 touch-downs.

1888. Univ. of Pa., o ; Yale, 54 points.

1889. Univ. of Pa., 10 points ; Yale, 20 points.

1890. Univ. of Pa., o ; Yale, 60 points.

1891. Univ. of Pa., o ; Yale, 48 points.

1892. Univ. of Pa., o ; Yale, 28 points.

1893. Univ. of Pa., 6 points ; Yale, 14 points.

1894. No game.

1895. No game.

UNIVERSITY OF PENNSYLVANIA–PRINCETON.

1876. Univ. of Pa., o ; Princeton, 6.

1878. Univ. of Pa., o ; Princeton, 2 goals, 4 touch-downs.

1879. Univ. of Pa., 11 safeties ; Princeton, 6 goals, 4 touch-downs.

1880. Univ. of Pa., 1 safety ; Princeton, 1 goal, 3 safeties.

1881. Univ. of Pa., 4 safeties ; Princeton, 4 goals, 6 touch-downs.

1882. Univ. of Pa., o ; Princeton, 10 goals, 4 touch-downs.

1883. Univ. of Pa., 6 points ; Princeton, 39 points.

1884. Univ. of Pa., o ; Princeton, 30 points.

1885. Univ. of Pa., 0 ; Princeton, 57 points.

1886. Univ. of Pa., 6 points ; Princeton, 28 points.

1887. Univ. of Pa., 0 ; Princeton, 96 points.

1888. Univ. of Pa., 0 ; Princeton, 4 points.

1889. Univ. of Pa., 4 points ; Princeton, 72 points.

1890. Univ. of Pa., 0 ; Princeton, 6 points.

1891. Univ. of Pa., 0 ; Princeton, 24 points.

1892. Univ. of Pa., 6 points ; Princeton, 4 points.

1893. Univ. of Pa., 0 ; Princeton, 4 points.

1894. Univ. of Pa., 12 ; Princeton, 0.

1895. No game.

HARVARD–CORNELL.

1891. Harvard, 77 ; Cornell, 0.

1892. Harvard, 20 ; Cornell, 14.

1893. Harvard, 34 ; Cornell, 0.

1894. Harvard, 22 ; Cornell, 12.

1895. Harvard, 25 ; Cornell, 0.

PRINCETON–CORNELL.

1893. Princeton, 46 ; Cornell, 0.

1894. Princeton, 12 ; Cornell, 4.

1895. Princeton, 6; Cornell, 0.

UNIVERSITY OF PENNSYLVANIA–CORNELL.

1893. Univ. of Pa., 50 ; Cornell, 0.

1894. Univ. of Pa., 6 ; Cornell, 0.

1895. Univ. of Pa., 46 ; Cornell, 2.

A PRIMER OF COLLEGE FOOTBALL

By W. H. LEWIS. Illustrated from Instantaneous Photographs and with Diagrams. 16mo. (*In Press.*)

Mr. Lewis, an old Harvard football centre-rush has put together in this book the result of his experiences in practical football. The work, therefore, is not so much a treatise on the game as a series of practical suggestions to be used by captains in teaching their men and coaching their teams. The book is divided respectively into the " individual," and "team" play. The part on the "individual" discusses, first, the individual plays, such as passing, kicking, running, falling on the ball and so on, and then the work of the individual players themselves. The second part discusses, first, offensive and then defensive team play. It will be seen, therefore, that the book is unique of its kind, and in its small compass will be eminently suited for use from day to day in the field or during the discussion after practice.

Published by HARPER & BROTHERS, New York.

☞ *For sale by all booksellers, or will be sent by the publishers, postage prepaid, on receipt of price.*

FOOTBALL FACTS AND FIGURES.

Compiled by WALTER CAMP. Post 8vo, Ornamental Paper Covers. (*Just Ready.*)

STATISTICS COLLECTED BY

The Hon. JAMES W. ALEXANDER, of the Equitable Life Assurance Company.

The Rev. JOSEPH H. TWICHELL, of the Yale Corporation.

The Hon. HENRY E. HOWLAND, of the New York Bar.

WALTER CAMP.

The Rev. ENDICOTT PEABODY, of Groton School.

ROBERT BACON, of the Harvard Board of Overseers.

This volume embodies the results of careful and painstaking inquiries as to the effects, physical and otherwise, of football, upon those taking part in the game. Information and statistics have been gathered from those best qualified to supply them—expert and celebrated players, members of the faculties of our colleges, etc.—and the work throws a flood of light upon a much-discussed subject.

PUBLISHED BY

HARPER & BROTHERS, New York

☞ *The above work is for sale by all booksellers, or will be sent by the publishers, postage prepaid, to any part of the United States, Canada, or Mexico, on receipt of the price.*

www.ingramcontent.com/pod-product-compliance
Lightning Source LLC
Chambersburg PA
CBHW020507270326
41926CB00008B/778